The Young Astronomer's Handbook

James Muirden

The Young
Astronomer's Handbook

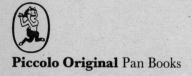

Piccolo Original Pan Books

for Daniel and Emma

First published 1977 by Pan Books Ltd,
Cavaye Place, London SW10 9PG
© James Muirden 1977
ISBN 0 330 25189 9
Filmset in 'Monophoto' Baskerville 12 on 14 pt and
printed in Great Britain by
Richard Clay (The Chaucer Press), Ltd, Bungay, Suffolk

Contents

1 The things we see in the sky

Imagine what life would be like if the world we live in were always covered with cloud. We should awake to grey mornings and go to bed in the dark and sombre nightfall. It would be a cheerless existence indeed. Short of going up above the clouds in an aeroplane we should have no idea of what causes day and night, or of the sort of universe we live in. In fact, we should know absolutely nothing at all about anything that wasn't right in front of our eyes, on the Earth's surface.

Perhaps, in other parts of the universe, there are people living lives like that, cut off from all knowledge of other things by the clouds that swirl over their heads. Suppose that one day, after hundreds or thousands of years of grey impenetrable skies, their clouds suddenly cleared towards nightfall. They would see a brilliant, overwhelming object – their sun – sinking towards the horizon. They would be terrified and fascinated, amazed and intrigued. Then their sun would set, and the sky would darken, and at first a few, then dozens, then hundreds or thousands of stars would shine out. Such a sight would overwhelm them, and they would probably run around thinking that they had gone mad.

Well, such glories and mysteries are free to us fortunate Earth-dwellers, and because they are free most people don't bother to consider them and go around in their own cloudy worlds with their eyes fixed on the ground. Astronomers are people who make the most of this fortunate chance that we live on a planet which generally has a clear sky. The window to the universe is open, and who can resist the temptation to peep out? Probably everyone has peeped out, just for a minute or two, on some sparkling night – but it seems so confusing that they have closed the window again, convinced that it is all beyond their comprehension.

Isn't this giving up a little too easily? Of course we can't really comprehend the vastness of space, but we can still learn enough to make the night sky a friendly rather than a baffling place. After all, the universe began long before our world came into existence, and it will be there long after this planet is cold, dark and dead; what a pity not to know something about it all!

So let us go out on an imaginary expedition, and find a hilltop with a good view all round, and wait for the Sun to set. We needn't take anything with us, although in a real-life expedition of this sort a pair of binoculars would always be useful. The point of this imaginary journey, though, is to take a fresh look at the things that everybody can see in the sky if they care to cast their eyes upwards.

When we reach our observation site, somewhere out in

the country where there are no town lights to hide the fainter stars, the Sun has nearly set and the sky is a deep blue. What is this blinding, searing object that we must never look directly at, called the Sun? It is a star, our own star, the star around which the Earth and the eight other planets that form the Solar System move. From our point of view, the Sun and the Earth are the most important objects in the universe. Without them, life would be impossible. The Earth gives us a platform to stand on, air to breathe and water to drink, and the Sun gives us heat. We could not survive without these things. If the Sun were not there, the Earth would be a frozen dead world, spinning through eternal night.

But when we look at the universe from an astronomical point of view, the picture is different. We see a huge gathering of stars: stars in clusters of thousands, or on their own, or even in pairs revolving around each other. We see bright stars and dim stars, small and large, white-hot or glowing red. We see young stars, barely shining yet, emerging from their birth-clouds of gas; adult stars sending out a steady beam as they have been doing for perhaps thousands of millions of years; and, almost unnoticed because they are so dim, we find dying stars that are cooling and flickering out – the embers of old suns.

The Sun and its planets lie somewhere among this throng. No cosmic eye would pick it out as being anything special. It is just one star among hundreds of millions, of average brightness. A microscope would be needed to detect the nine tiny specks of dust revolving around it, and no one could guess that on the third speck from the centre people were gazing up at the sky and wondering about it all!

So our Sun is a very ordinary body to everyone except ourselves. But now from our observation site we watch it sinking to the west. This motion of the Sun across the sky is another illusion, for it is really the Earth that is moving, not the Sun. The Earth spins round on its axis once in twenty-four hours, moving in a west-to-east direction. This makes the Sun, Moon, planets and stars appear to rise in the east and set in the west.

Once the Sun has set below the horizon, we are in a period of twilight that lasts until the sky is completely dark. Twilight is an exciting time. The objects which shine in the night sky are up there all the time, but the blue veil of the sky hides them. As the sky darkens, so they are revealed. We watch and wait, and keep an eye out for the first sparkling points of light.

The first one is seen very soon after sunset, high up in the west over the place where the Sun has set. This is Venus, one of the planets in our Solar System. It looks like a star, but no star appears as bright as this in the sky. This is because it is closer to the Sun than we are and receives more light, while its cloudy atmosphere reflects light very well. Venus is never very far from the Sun in our sky, sometimes rising before dawn in the east, and some months later setting after sunset in the west. Apart from the Moon, Venus is the Earth's closest neighbour in space, and like all the planets it shines by reflecting the Sun's light.

As the colour of the sky deepens the first stars come out. Two or three bright ones are the first seen. How faint they seem, after the Sun! The slightest breath of blue sky is enough to hide most of them, and yet almost all of the twinkling points that are now coming into view are really brighter, or more **luminous**, than the Sun. This tells us that they must be very far away indeed. Now the last light goes out of the sky, and the stars shine forth in their full splendour. We spend a few minutes gazing at them. What do we notice? We could draw up a list of several points:

1 The stars are slowly drifting across the sky, from east to west.
2 There are very bright stars that can be seen in the early twilight, and faint ones that show only when the sky is completely dark – and others in between these extremes.
3 Most of the stars seem to be white, but some show a yellow or orange tint.

These observations are all easy to make, but if we think about them carefully we may learn something. The first point, of course, is just an illusion; the rotating Earth is carrying us around with it so that our view into space is changing and making the stars *appear* to move. But why should some stars appear bright and others faint? One possible explanation is that they are all at the same distance from us, but some are really more luminous than others (just as a bright electric lamp will outshine a torch bulb set up alongside it). Another explanation is that they are all equally luminous but are at different distances from us, so that the ones that are furthest away appear faintest. Or it could be a bit of both.

Ancient astronomers believed the first explanation. They thought that the Earth was at the centre of the universe and that the stars were attached to the inside of a huge invisible ball, or sphere, that rotated around the Earth once a day. Ideas changed greatly after 1608 when the invention of the telescope revealed the marvels of the night sky. Astronomers, on the whole, were then more inclined to believe that each star was much the same as any other, and that their different brightnesses in the sky was an effect of distance, the brightest stars being those closest to us. It was not until about a century ago that stars were found to differ greatly among themselves, and a picture of the universe as we now see it began to emerge.

We now know that all the stars we see in the sky, whether using the naked eye or a telescope, are fiercely shining bodies much larger than the Earth (the Sun itself is a hundred times the diameter of our planet). Some stars are so hot that if they changed places with the Sun, life on Earth would wither and die, and the oceans would boil away. Others are so much dimmer and cooler than the Sun that the exchange would freeze us. The Sun is about average, in size and temperature, for a star. It is slightly yellow in tint; pure white stars are hotter, and the yellow and reddish stars that we see in the sky have cooler surfaces. Astronomers have now measured the distances of many stars. Even the nearest one to us is about 270,000 times as far away as the Sun, and most are hundreds or even thousands of times further away than this!

Such huge distances cannot be measured conveniently in kilometres. Even the distance of the Earth from the Sun (a very useful distance, known as the Astronomical Unit) is about 150 million kilometres. When we start talking of the distances to the stars, even this unit is tiny. Instead, astronomers tend to use light-years. A beam of light travels through space at about 300,000 kilometres a second; that is, once round the Earth in about an eighth of a second. In a year it would cover over nine million million kilometres, and this is the distance that astronomers know as a light-year. The nearest star is about four and a third light-years away.

Compared with these enormous distances, all the planets that go to form the Earth's neighbours in the Solar System are very, very close indeed. The Sun and its nine planets (among which the Earth stands midway in size) form a tiny island in the unimaginable emptiness of space. In the night sky they all appear equally remote from us because our eyes cannot tell distances greater than a few kilometres. So let us shrink everything to a scale that can be understood, and start off with the Sun as a ball ten centimetres across, about the size of an orange. In the Solar System, the Earth would be indicated by a pinhead just under one millimetre across, at a distance of eleven metres from the orange. The inner planets, Mercury and Venus, would be closer to the orange, while the outer ones (Mars, Jupiter, Saturn, Uranus and Neptune) would lie between the orbit of the Earth and that of Pluto, the outermost planet, another pinhead about 420 metres from the orange. To show the nearest star, however, we should have to set up another orange 3,000 kilometres away! On this scale, the whole bulk of the real Earth could contain only thirty orange-sized stars.

We can see from this model that stars count for much more than planets in the astronomical scene. It is only because the other planets in the Solar System are so close to us that we can see most of them with the naked eye. If the nearest star had a planetary family revolving around it, no telescope could hope to make out anything of it. To us, however, Venus and Jupiter, and sometimes Mars, appear brighter than any star, even though they are only reflecting the Sun's light. Mercury and Saturn are also naked-eye objects, and so is Uranus if the sky is very clear. Only the outermost planets, Neptune and Pluto, require a telescope for their detection.

So how can we tell the difference between the multitudes of stars and the few nearby planets? A powerful telescope will show all the planets, except for distant Pluto, as little discs, while the stars are so far away that they appear only as points of light. Yet the ancient astronomers, centuries before telescopes were even thought of, had distinguished the brighter planets. They were able to do this because the planets move around the sky, while the stars do not.

Now we must make sure that we are not confused by the word 'move'. The celestial objects appear to move from east to west as if they were fastened to the inside of some huge rotating sphere, as the ancients believed. This is the movement caused by the rotation of the Earth. We call it daily motion because this is the same motion that makes the Sun appear to move across the sky, giving us day and night.

Ignoring this daily motion, however, we find that the stars still form the same patterns in relation to each other. This is not because they are really standing still in space. Some are moving at speeds of many kilometres a second. But they are so far away that even these tremendous speeds do not make the patterns change noticeably, even over centuries of time. The constellations that we see today are the same imaginary figures that early astronomers drew among the stars of their night skies.

The planets are much closer to us than are the stars, and they are moving at speeds of several kilometres a second around the Sun. So, as they move along their orbits, they change their positions against the starry background. Thousands of years ago, the shepherd-astronomers of the Middle East noticed that no less than five of the 'stars' in the sky moved about, and the word planet comes from their word for 'wanderer'. The planets were identified by their motion and named after various figures in the mythology of those times, long before anybody knew for certain what they were. Because the orbits of the planets lie in almost the same plane (as if they had been drawn on a sheet of paper), they keep to a distinct belt, or zone, in the sky. This is known as the **Zodiac**.

None of the planets moves fast enough for its motion to be noticed with the naked eye in just a few hours, unless perhaps it lies in the same direction as a bright star. But if you were to make a map of all the bright stars and compare it with the sky a fortnight later, you would find that one, two, or even three of these 'stars' had moved. These would be the planets Mars, Jupiter and Saturn. Venus we already recognize because it is always near the sunset or sunrise part of the sky and is very bright, while Mercury keeps even closer to the Sun and will probably not be found except by a special search.

What else can we see and learn about on our imaginary evening? We know the difference between planets and stars, and how to tell them apart. Can we find out

Figure 1 This is the outline our Milky Way Galaxy would show if we could see it edge-on. The Sun and its planets lie about halfway from the centre to the edge. The Sun is just one of thousands of millions of stars in our Galaxy

anything about how the stars are arranged in space? Are they scattered in disorder, or in small groups, or in great clusters? We shall find out more later on, but another useful naked-eye observation can be made now. If the night is really dark, a pale, irregular band of light will be seen crossing the sky through some of the star-patterns. This is the Milky Way (*figure 1*). With binoculars or a telescope this band turns into a multitude of faint stars, so close and dim that to the unaided eye they form a glowing cloud. If we look away from the Milky Way, we see far fewer stars. The explanation for this is that the stars are arranged in a flattened cluster, rather like two saucers clapped together with their rims touching. Our Sun lies somewhere inside this cluster. When we look at the Milky Way we are looking through the longest direction in the cluster, where the stars recede to a tremendous distance. Away from the Milky Way we are seeing fewer stars before the edge is reached. This whole enormous grouping of about 100,000 million stars is called our **Galaxy**.

And beyond the Galaxy? Binoculars and telescopes reveal tiny, wispy patches of light shining far off in the depths of space. These are other galaxies, some like our own, others different. These galaxies of stars make up what we know as the universe. Each one contains thousands of millions of stars, but they are so distant that only one or two can be seen with the unaided eye. This is a breathtaking thought when we realize that each of those stars, on average, is about as bright as the Sun!

The stars are the building-blocks of the universe. Stars make up galaxies, and planets belong to stars. Let us take a look at the star closest to us: the Sun.

2 The Sun: our powerhouse

How does the Sun keep shining? That is one of the biggest problems astronomers have had to solve. No process that we have been able to invent for supplying power, heat and electricity comes anywhere near to matching the Sun for power-packed performance.

At our distance (150 million kilometres) from the Sun, only about a two thousand millionth of our star's total energy strikes the Earth. Even so, if we could collect all this light and heat and use it to drive electric generators, we should find ourselves with several thousand times more energy than is needed. In fact, the Sun manufactures as much energy as we do in a year, in only three millionths of a second!

We know something else that is almost as remarkable. In the Earth's rocks are records of fossils that show that life has existed here for about three thousand million years. In all that time the Sun's power cannot have changed very much, or the Earth's surface would have boiled or been frozen, and life would have come to an abrupt end.

This amazing power is one of the keys to understanding how the universe works. The Sun is a star, and if there were no stars everything would be cold, dark and dead. If we can understand how the Sun operates it probably explains how other stars shine as well. It is not surprising that studies of the Sun have formed one of the most important branches of astronomy, since all the other stars in the Galaxy are so far away that not one of them can be seen as anything but a point of light.

The Sun is so close to us that it appears as a large disc to the naked eye. Now is the time to say a few words about observing the Sun. Most people have had the unpleasant experience of being burnt on the hand or arm with a 'burning glass', which is nothing more than a magnifying glass that forms a concentrated image of the Sun on your skin. After a second or two you give a yelp of pain, because that tiny image is hotter than the temperature of boiling water.

If you look at the Sun, the lens in your eye acts as a burning glass and the tiny, concentrated image will partly or completely destroy the sensitive screen, or **retina**, in the eye on which is formed your image of the world. This retina is so delicate that it can be hurt long before any feeling of pain makes you turn away, and this damage will probably be permanent. Our awesome star is something to be treated with the greatest respect. Certainly there are safe ways of observing it, and we shall mention one in Chapter 10, but the general rule must be NEVER to look directly at the Sun at all.

The real diameter of the disc that shines in our sky is 1,392,000 kilometres. This is 109 times the diameter of the Earth. If we wanted to fill this disc with full-scale copies of our planet, we should need over a million of them. The interesting thing is that if the Sun and this huge pile of Earths could be weighed separately on some gigantic set of scales, the pile of Earths would be found to be four times heavier than the Sun.

So the Sun cannot be built out of matter that is as heavy as the rocks and metals that make up the Earth. Its composing materials must be much lighter than that. In fact, the Sun is made up mostly of the lightest gas in the universe, hydrogen – the gas that early balloonists used to carry them to dizzy heights in our atmosphere.

The idea of the Sun being made up of gas is a little difficult to understand. We think of gas as invisible, formless stuff, while the Sun is a hard-edged, round ball. But the Sun isn't as simple as it looks, and it extends much further, too. Every now and then, the Moon passes right in front of the Sun and blocks out the shining disc. This is called a total solar **eclipse**. When this happens, the daytime sky is almost as dark as night for the seconds or minutes that the eclipse lasts, and we can see the Sun's outer region, the **corona**, shining like the petals of a huge flower around the black disc of the Moon. As soon as the Moon passes on and the Sun shines out again, the corona is drowned in the daylight glare, but it is there all the time. And it is huge – many millions of kilometres across.

This corona, which is thousands of times thinner than our own air, is the Sun's outer atmosphere. The surface we normally see is the point at which the gas is dense enough to form a shining layer known as the

photosphere. We cannot see anything below the photosphere, but by making observations of this surface and the layers above, astronomers have been able to build up a likely picture of how the Sun shines.

Let us go back in time, and try to imagine how the Sun, or any other star, came into existence. It must have had a beginning, and one day it must end; and by looking at other stars in the Galaxy, astronomers are convinced that the Sun began as nothing more than a huge cold cloud of matter, mostly hydrogen gas, perhaps thirty times as big as the whole Solar System. These particles began to fall together, first into clumps of just a few, then into bigger clumps, then into just a few dense clouds that came together, collapsing into a smaller and smaller space as the attraction due to that strange, universal force known as **gravity** grew stronger.

All matter is made up of tiny particles known as **atoms** – bodies so small that a matchbox-full of air contains millions of them. These atoms are dancing freely around, colliding with each other and bouncing away. The thinner the gas, the further apart the atoms are and the less frequently they collide. If you take a sample of gas and reduce the size of its container, the atoms are forced closer together so that they collide with each other more frequently. These collisions give off energy, usually as heat. A common example of this is forcing more air into a bicycle tyre: the pump gets hot. Similarly, as the solar cloud condensed, it became hot and started to glow with the heat, at first shining redly but becoming yellow as the temperature rose. When this happened the collapse slowed down and stopped, because the radiation being produced at the searing centre of the young Sun started forcing the outer layers back outwards again.

If this were the process by which the Sun shone, the star would have gradually cooled down, reducing the energy production so that more collapse could begin, releasing more energy . . . and so on. Finally it would have reached a point where the gas could collapse no more because it was solid, and the star would cool right down and die. But this cannot be the answer because such a collapse would be over in just a few million years, much less time than life has existed on our planet.

Not until about forty years ago did scientists really find out what must be happening inside the Sun, and the answer seems to lie in the way that matter is built up. Everything that we can touch or see in the universe, from the stones beneath our feet to the remotest stars, is made up from one or more of a known number of **elements**. Altogether, ninety-two elements seem to occur naturally, though it is possible to manufacture a few other very unstable ones, such as plutonium. Common examples of elements are the gases hydrogen and oxygen (oxygen and another element, nitrogen, make up most of the air we breathe), and the solids iron and carbon.

Now, although all the elements are different from each other, their atoms are made up of the same ingredients – protons, neutrons and electrons. Protons and electrons are very light, with positive and negative electric charges. Neutrons have no electric charge but give the atom most of its mass. By altering its atomic structure, it is possible to turn one element into another. When this happens, an enormous amount of energy can be given out. It is called **nuclear energy**, and on Earth we have found out how to use it, in a small way, in electricity generating plants and, of course, the hydrogen bomb.

Nuclear energy processes that have been used by

scientists take place at temperatures of a few million degrees Centigrade (°C). When the Sun contracted, the temperature at its centre, or core, probably reached about seventeen million degrees, and the hydrogen started being changed, or transmuted, into another element, helium. Once begun, this process gives out enough energy to keep itself going, and there is so much hydrogen present that scientists expect the Sun to keep shining for many thousands of millions of years yet. The four and a half thousand million years of its past life are quite short compared with the age that we expect it to reach.

Of course, nobody has ever been inside the Sun to find out if this hydrogen-helium process is really the one that keeps it shining. But it explains so many things that we observe, both in the Sun and in its fellow stars, that nobody really doubts that this is the right answer. Scientific knowledge is built up by putting forward theories (which usually cannot ever really be proved) to explain facts that everybody agrees about.

Sometimes, new facts are discovered that prove a theory to have been wrong because the old facts were wrong, and so a new theory has to be put forward. For instance, a hundred years ago scientists were happy to believe that gravitational contraction could explain why the Sun shines, simply because the Solar System was thought to be just a few million years old. When the Earth was found to be much older than this, the theory collapsed. A new observation could suddenly make scientists wonder if their ideas about the Sun are right even now. In fact, at this very moment there are doubts as to whether the Sun's core is really hot enough to produce the hydrogen-helium transmutation, and much discussion and calculation is going on. The point is, though, that nobody has yet come up with a better explanation of how the Sun and the stars produce their energy, and there are very many observations that support it.

So we have a picture of the Sun as a huge ball of gas, mostly hydrogen, that is slowly being turned into helium. This helium forms a slowly-growing central core, and in Chapter 6 we shall see what may happen to the Sun in future ages. For the moment, however, what of the parts of the Sun that we *can* observe, from the surface or photosphere (temperature about 5,800°C) outwards?

The Italian observer Galileo was one of the first people to look at the Sun with a telescope, in the year 1609. He was surprised to see that the disc was sometimes sprinkled with dark spots. The nature of these **sunspots** is still something of a mystery, even though they have been observed now for centuries. One thing that we do know is that although the spots themselves last only for a few days or weeks, the Sun shows periods of high sunspot activity every eleven years or so. This is the **sunspot cycle**. Between the times of greatest activity, sunspot numbers are low and the disc may appear completely unmarked for several days at a time. The year 1976 saw the Sun at minimum activity, after a maximum in 1969. The maximum before that one, in 1957, produced more sunspot activity than had ever been observed before. Nobody knows why the Sun should have this cycle of activity, but we can look forward to good sunspot activity round about the year 1980.

Another strange thing about the outbreak of sunspots is that they do not scatter themselves in a disorderly way over the Sun's surface. They keep to definite belts or zones

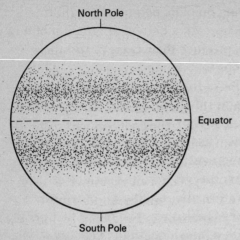

North Pole

Equator

South Pole

Figure 2 The darkest shading shows the parts of the Sun where most sunspots are seen. Fewer occur in the lighter shading, and hardly any are ever seen elsewhere

on the globe (*figure 2*), rarely appearing near the Sun's equator, and never at the poles. Once again, this is an occurrence that has not been explained.

Since the spots are part of the photosphere, the Sun's rotation on its axis carries them around with it. If we observe a spot near the Sun's centre, and keep watch on it, it will have reached the western edge or **limb** of the Sun a week later. If it survives long enough another fortnight will find it reappearing at the eastern limb after its passage around the hidden hemisphere, and four weeks (more accurately, twenty-seven days) after the first observation it will be found once more near the Sun's centre. This is the time it takes for our star to rotate once on its axis, as seen from the Earth. Interestingly, the Sun does not rotate like a solid body, and the regions near the poles take two or three days longer to turn once than the parts nearer the equator, where the sunspots usually appear.

What are these curious spots? They seem to be huge regions of the photosphere where, for some reason, the gases are in violent motion up and down. Because most of these gases are cooler than the photosphere, with a temperature of perhaps 4,000°C, the spots appear to be dark because they give out much less light. But they are still brighter than the surfaces of some of the stars that shine in the night sky! Most spots, when examined closely, show two regions: a dark centre or **umbra** and a more lightly shaded border or **penumbra**, indicating regions of different motion and temperature (*figure 3*). The cause of sunspots is thought to lie in disturbances deep below the photosphere.

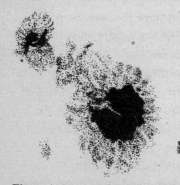

Figure 3 A sunspot like this one is many times larger than the Earth

The gases in a sunspot are whirling round at speeds of up to two kilometres a second, which is perhaps forty times as fast as the highest winds ever recorded on the Earth. But because they are so huge and far away, sunspots seem to develop quite slowly. Our first sight of a new spot shows one or two tiny dark marks or **pores** just a few hundred kilometres across. These enlarge and spread over the following days until the group may extend over an area many times that of the Earth. Large features such as this can take several months to die away, but most normal spots last not more than a few weeks. Drawing sunspots and watching their development and decay is a very interesting part of astronomy: you never know what to expect next.

Sunspots are easy to observe, but other important features of the Sun are more elusive. Soaring up from the photosphere at speeds of several hundred kilometres a second, **prominences** are among the most violent objects we can observe in the universe. Some of these tremendous surges of hot hydrogen gas could swallow a hundred Earths. But to see them we need one of the rarest of all natural happenings: a total eclipse of the Sun.

The Sun and our Moon are of very different sizes. The Sun is almost exactly 400 times the diameter of the Moon but it is also about 400 times as far away, so that they both appear the same size in the sky. This means that if the Moon happens to pass in front of the Sun it can completely block out the solar disc, giving us a total eclipse.

Prominences are bright, but the glare of the photosphere is much brighter and usually drowns them. During a total eclipse, when the day sky suddenly darkens to twilight (and a wonderful experience it is!), all this glare is snatched away and any prominences at the limb of the Sun can be seen as rosy-coloured spots or spikes shining at the edge of the black outline of the Moon. At the same time we see the Sun's outer atmosphere, the

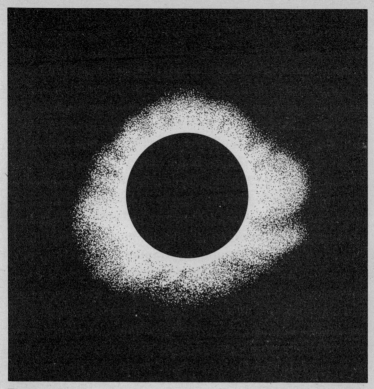

Figure 4 This drawing of a total eclipse of the Sun shows its atmosphere, the corona, shining out around the black outline of the Moon

corona, that also is usually hidden by the daylight glare. Even with the naked eye the corona can be seen to extend for two million kilometres or more from the edge of the Sun. In fact, we know that some atomic particles are being thrown out even further from the Sun in such large numbers that they can be detected by special instruments in satellites and space probes. This **solar wind** seems to extend right through the inner part of the Solar System, as a great outpouring of material.

27

The Sun's photosphere, then, is a turmoil of activity. Outbreaks of sometimes enormous spots blot its surface. Surging prominences can erupt for tens of thousands of kilometres. The solar wind pours outwards. And behind all this, as steady as the solid old planet on which we live, its colossal output of heat and light streams on.

Light and heat! Without the Sun's light we could not see; we should have to live by starlight, for the Moon, too, would be extinguished and could be seen only as a black shape against the stars. But, more important, vegetation could not grow without light. Astronomers believe that the Earth's atmosphere, in the early days of its existence, contained very little of the life-giving gas oxygen but a great deal of the stifling gas carbon dioxide (a compound of carbon and oxygen). The leaves of plants absorb carbon dioxide, using the carbon for cell-building purposes and releasing oxygen, and over countless millions of years the oxygen content of the atmosphere was increased until it could support the advanced life-forms of today. To perform this essential task, plants need light.

Heat is just as important as light. A body taken out into the gulf of space, far from any star, would cool down until its temperature was about 270°C below zero. (Zero, or 0°C, is the freezing point of water.) At this temperature, atomic particles practically come to a halt and most materials are 'dead'. Without the Sun's heat, our atmosphere would collapse, frozen solid, to the ground, and the Earth would be as dead a world as anyone could imagine.

Light and heat are different varieties of the same thing: **electromagnetic radiation**. We shall just call it

'radiation' for short. Radiation is the energy given out
when a body is heated, and it is caused by the atoms in
the body becoming activated or excited. The type of
radiation given out by the body depends on how excited
the atoms are, and this in turn depends on how hot the
body is.

We can heat a body in many ways. A very convenient
way, if, for example, it is a piece of metal wire, is to pass
an electric current through it. We begin by passing
through a very weak current. The wire hardly feels warm
to the touch, but it has already begun to give off very low-
energy radiation. A radio set would pick up this radiation
as a hum. With more current the wire becomes
uncomfortably warm and then hot. It is now emitting
higher-energy radiation that we call heat, and the
sensitive nerves in our skin can detect it. A little more
current, and the wire begins to glow a dull red; it is now
beginning to emit visible light as well as heat waves and
radio waves. As the current is turned up still more, the red
turns to yellow, then white, then blue (in fact, the wire
would have burned up before this last stage was reached
because the white-hot metal would have combined with
the oxygen in the air and vaporized).

If our wire could survive even more energy being
passed through it we should find it emitting the rather
dangerous ultra-violet radiation, which causes sunburn
and can destroy skin cells, and then the really lethal
gamma-rays and X-rays, which pass through the body
and can cause death.

The Sun, whose surface is far hotter than our piece of
wire could ever be, emits all these radiations; from
invisible radio waves to warming heat rays, to visible light

29

waves, and finally to the furious, killing high-energy waves. The Sun is the sort of star that can do a bit of everything in the way of radiation. Later, we shall mention very cool red stars that emit little or nothing in the way of high-energy radiation, and fiercely hot blue stars that pour out huge doses of lethal rays. Even so, the Sun's high-energy radiation is enough to stop all life from developing on the Earth's surface if it were not cut out by an invisible layer high in the atmosphere, and travellers into space must take special precautions to protect themselves.

Sometimes, just to show that it is not to be taken for granted, the Sun raises its voice, and from the disturbed turmoil of its surface, where the sunspots break out, it pours forth great bursts of radiation. Sometimes the scene of these cataclysms – or **flares** – is seen as a brilliant patch on the photosphere lasting for just a few minutes. When this extra radiation reaches the Earth, the atoms in the highest layers of our atmosphere may begin to glow, giving displays of shimmering light known as the **aurora** in the night sky. At the same time a lower layer known as the **ionosphere**, which is used as a reflector for long-distance radio communication, may be destroyed for several hours. When this happens, distant radio stations suffer a fade-out. These events happen most often near the time of maximum sunspot activity, but even near the minimum period of its cycle the Sun can make itself heard!

The Sun is our star. In the beginning it gave us our birth; now it nurses us in its light and warmth. What of the little group of bodies in its family, the Solar System?

3 The Sun's family: the Solar System

If we could see the Sun as it was five thousand million years ago, a strange scene would meet our eyes. We should see a vast, tide-rent black cloud, flattened like a thin lens and rotating around a young, cool star seen only dimly through the swirling wisps and tatters of matter. In this black nebula, extending for thousands of millions of kilometres into space, is all the material that will soon condense into the planets of our Solar System. Hydrogen and oxygen to make water for our seas and rivers; nitrogen for our atmosphere; silicon for rocks; carbon for green leaves, tree trunks, coal and oil, and living cells; iron with which to forge tools . . . everything that will one day go to make our green and blue planet is hidden in this dark fog, as well as the materials for the eight neighbour planets of Earth.

A few million years pass before we visit the scene again. Now everything is clearer. The Sun has come up to full power on its nuclear engine, and shines bright and yellow. The cloud, too, is changed. Instead of a chaotic disc we find in the clearing haze a number of black cloudlets of solid particles. Some orbit singly around the Sun; others form groups, gradually merging together and growing in size.

We depart again. On our next visit, after further ages have passed, the haze has gone. Nine objects are circling the Sun; they are still cloudy, but solid enough to have surfaces of a sort, and now very hot. The cloudlets that we saw have been attracted together, and the remaining haze has been drawn to these young planets or thrown out of the Solar System altogether by the Sun's radiation. As the infant worlds condense tightly under the force of gravity, they begin to heat up like little stars. The difference is that none of them, not even the giant planet Jupiter, can become hot enough for nuclear reactions to begin, because they do not contain enough material to push the central pressure sufficiently high. Even so, they become hot enough for the metals in the material – particularly iron and nickel – to melt and fall to the centre, forming a core.

But what of the commonest atoms of all in the nebula, those of hydrogen? Hydrogen is the lightest gas of all, and it can easily escape into space. The gravity of the inner four planets – Mercury, Venus, Earth and Mars – was too small for them to hold on to any free hydrogen, although, in the case of the Earth, a good deal combined with oxygen to form water for the oceans and rainfall. But the next four planets – Jupiter, Saturn, Uranus and Neptune – are giants, with huge gravitational pulls. They have held on to a great deal of hydrogen, and to this day they are wreathed in the gas and its compounds with other elements. This is the greatest difference between the four inner planets and the next four giant planets, and it has happened mainly because of their size. The outermost planet, Pluto, is smaller than Earth, and has a very thin, frozen atmospheric covering. The three outer planets, Uranus, Neptune and Pluto, were discovered during the past two centuries, but they have been given the names of Roman gods to fit in with the names of the other planets.

All this happened thousands of millions of years ago. The oldest rocks found on the Moon, which probably give the time when our satellite had cooled enough to form a crust over its molten mass, are about four and a half thousand million years old. We cannot find such ancient rocks on the Earth's surface, but this is probably because they were re-melted in later volcanic upheavals. Since that time, the surfaces of the planets have cooled down, although their cores are probably still very hot. The only warmth that they enjoy now is what comes from the Sun, and their surface temperatures go all the way from about 480°C for smouldering Venus (above the melting-point of lead) to about minus 230°C for Pluto, which is not much warmer than deep interstellar space.

The planets were not the only bodies to be formed from the solar nebula. Other worlds, just a few hundred or thousand kilometres across, came into being. Some of these were captured by the gravitational pull of the planets and went into orbit around them instead of around the Sun. These are satellites. All of the planets except Mercury, Venus and Pluto have at least one known satellite or moon. Other small bodies still orbit the Sun as very tiny worlds (the **minor planets**). Few of these are more than a hundred kilometres across, and most are much smaller. Nearly all circle the Sun between the orbits of Mars and Jupiter.

Astronomers, on the whole, believe the solar nebula theory of the origin of the Solar System, because it explains so many things about it. It seems practically certain that the Sun and planets were formed at around the same time, and from the same mixture of matter. One reason for liking the 'rotating disc' theory is that the planets all move around the Sun in the same direction, and their orbits lie in almost the same plane, instead of being mixed up at all sorts of angles. If the planets had been formed somewhere out in space, and then accidentally captured by the gravity of the Sun, the Solar System would be a confusion of ill-assorted bodies instead of the fairly orderly family that we see. No astronomer seriously believes that the planets are a chance collection of worlds, and this fact alone makes it seem very likely that there are many other solar systems in the Galaxy, probably with Earth-like planets and living forms like our own.

Another piece of evidence for organized creation is the fact that most of the planets move in orbits that are very nearly perfect circles (*figure 5*). None is exactly circular, however; each orbit is what we call an **ellipse**. An ellipse is the shape traced out when a pencil is drawn around inside a loop of cotton placed over two pins (*figure 6*). These pins mark the **foci** of the ellipse, and the farther apart they are, the more elongated or **eccentric** is the resulting ellipse. A circle is a special type of ellipse in which the two foci lie on top of each other. Each planet in the Solar System moves in an elliptical orbit, and the Sun lies in one focus. The Earth swings closest to the Sun

34

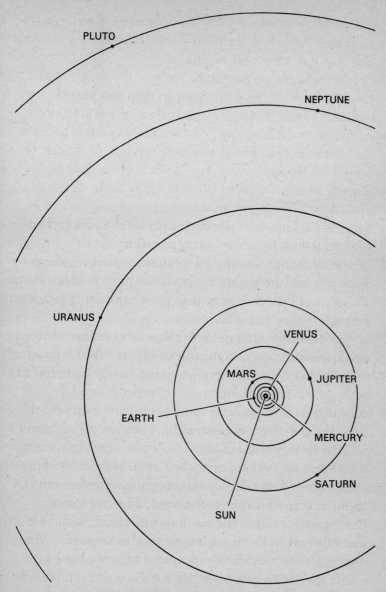

Figure 5 The circles show the orbits of the different planets in the
Solar System, indicating their different distances from the Sun

Figure 6 How to draw an ellipse

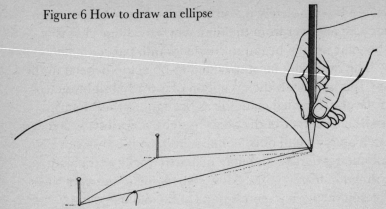

(a position known as **perihelion**) round about 4 January, and is farthest from the Sun (**aphelion**) about 3 July, but the difference is not enough to notice without making accurate measurements. Only on the planets Mercury and Pluto would the Sun appear to grow noticeably larger and smaller as they go on their way.

We have seen that the Solar System contains some very small worlds known as the minor planets. Many hundreds of them have been observed, shining faintly by reflected sunlight. Other and much tinier bodies, just a few centimetres or millimetres across, also move around the Sun. We call them **meteoroids**. They are far too small to be seen by reflected sunlight, but some move in eccentric orbits that carry them near the Earth. When this happens the meteoroid streaks down through the atmosphere at a speed of many kilometres a second. The tremendous heating effect causes the air in its path to glow and we see a brief streak of light: a **meteor** or 'shooting star'. Many meteoroids move in huge swarms, and when the Earth passes through a swarm we see a meteor shower. This is how we know of these minute bodies which otherwise

36

would be completely invisible. These tiny grains of matter may be left over from the time when the huge clouds of the solar nebula began to condense into particles.

The rarest but most spectacular object to be seen in the sky (perhaps with the exception of a really bright meteor or **fireball**, which could be as brilliant as the Moon) is another member of the Solar System, a **comet**. A comet is itself a very small object. The solid part is only a few kilometres across, and may be partly rocky and partly formed of frozen gases. Most comets spend much of their lives in the very remotest parts of the Solar System, beyond the orbit of Pluto and possibly even some distance towards the nearest stars. Even at this distance, however, the pull of the Sun attracts it. As years, centuries, or even periods of thousands of years pass, it slowly approaches, dim and unheralded. As it passes the orbits of the outer planets, it speeds up, flashing past the rest in a matter of weeks and whirling round the Sun, perhaps at a smaller distance even than the planet Mercury, in a day or two. The sudden intense heat turns its ice to gas, and the trapped dust in the ice is released. Its speed of movement, and the force of the solar wind, throw this matter back into a tail millions of kilometres long. For a few days this glorious sight shines in our sky, and then it steadily dims as the cooling comet returns to the frozen reaches of space.

Only a few comets every century are as bright as this, but there are many smaller ones that can be seen easily with a telescope or binoculars, and some never pass beyond the realm of the known planets. We shall have more to say about these mysterious bodies in Chapter 5, but first we must embark on a tour of the planets and satellites of the Solar System.

4 The planets: the Earth and its neighbours

We have already seen that there is a great difference between the four small inner planets and the next four giant planets. When they formed from the solar nebula, the giant planets held on to their supplies of hydrogen, which now forms the thick soup that we see today as their 'surfaces'. The inner planets probably never held on to any noticeable amounts of free hydrogen at all, and we encounter here the solid, rocky surfaces that formed as molten layers over their heavy iron cores. These rocks are formed mainly by the combination of the elements silicon, carbon, iron and oxygen, that were too heavy to escape into space when the planets condensed and warmed up.

Mercury: the innermost planet

Very few people have ever noticed this shy little world. It is never much more than an outspread hand's width away from the Sun, and we must look for it in deep twilight, over the Sun's place, in the morning or evening.

At its average distance of fifty-eight million kilometres, Mercury whirls around the Sun in only eighty-eight days.

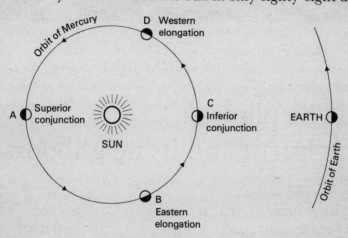

Figure 7 The movements and phases of Mercury. The upper diagram gives the names of the different positions as it revolves around the Sun. The lower diagram shows the phases we see at different positions

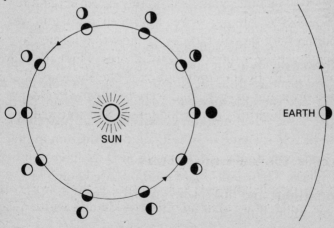

If it did not move as fast as this, it would be dragged down on to the Sun's surface. The further a planet is from the Sun, the longer is its 'year', or the time it takes to go around the Sun once, not only because its orbit is larger but because it is moving more slowly along the orbit. Compare Mercury's year of two and a half of our months with Pluto's year of two and a half of our centuries!

Astronomers have always found Mercury one of the most difficult planets to observe, because of the briefness of its appearances before vanishing back into the Sun's rays. Also, it is a small world only 4,880 kilometres across – less than half the diameter of the Earth – and to us it appears very small. At an average view, it is about the size of a penny piece seen from a distance of 520 metres. A very large telescope and good viewing conditions are essential, and even then not much can be seen.

Another difficulty in observing Mercury is that the planet passes through phases like the Moon. *Figure* 7 explains why. The Sun shines only on the half, or hemisphere, of a planet facing it. When Mercury is at position A, its day side is towards the Earth so that we should see a round disc – but we cannot see it because it is on the far side of the Sun, a position known as **superior conjunction**. When it has reached position B it is at its greatest distance from the Sun in the sky, but only half of its day side is visible and it looks like a half Moon. By the time it has reached position C (**inferior conjunction**), its night side is facing us, it is again near the Sun in the sky, and we cannot see it. At position D we have another half-phase. These half-phase positions are known as **elongations**, and this is when we have the best view – but of only half the disc!

So it is not surprising that we had to wait for the age of space probes before anything definite was known of what this planet looks like. The photographs sent back by the US vehicle *Mariner 10* in 1974 and 1975 showed for the first time that the surface of Mercury is very much like the Moon's, covered with craters and huge solidified flows of lava from the interior. In ages past, probably between three and four thousand million years ago, the young planet must have been bombarded by solid objects from space up to several kilometres across, just as the Moon must have been to produce the craters that we see today.

Over this airless world hangs the huge Sun, appearing nearly three times as large as the one we know, looming still larger at perihelion when the planet is only forty-six million kilometres away. Beneath its terrible glare the surface becomes as hot as the coal in a slow fire and lead would run as a liquid. But as the planet spins slowly on its axis, giving a day of fifty-eight and a half Earth days, these parts are carried into the night hemisphere and begin to cool down to the temperature of space, reaching about 170°C below zero before warming again in the dreadful sunrise. This huge drop happens because Mercury has no atmosphere to cloak in the heat. The surface of Venus is probably hotter than that of Mercury, and the outer planets are colder than Mercury's night, but none passes through anything like the changes experienced by this smallest of the planets.

Impact craters – round, saucer-shaped depressions, often larger than whole Earth cities, with walls thrown up higher than the surrounding plain and sometimes a central mountain as well – are a common feature of the innermost planets. When these worlds were formed, and the outer layers had cooled enough to form a thin, hard crust, other solid bodies whirling round the Sun could strike this crust and leave a scar. Of course, a planet offers a very small target in the huge wastes of space, but over millions and millions of years a great number of these impacts must have occurred, continuing until the larger projectiles had been used up. Most of the craters that we see on Mercury, the Moon, and Mars are probably older than three thousand million years, although the small pits just a few kilometres across are likely to be more recent.

These cratering impacts depend on having a supply of rocky missiles to do the damage, but a cooling planet can still have a violent surface. When it condenses, the heaviest metals like iron and nickel fall to the centre. Amongst these metals is found uranium, whose atoms undergo a steady change of structure due to a property known as **radioactivity**, and eventually turn into another element, lead. Radioactive change gives out energy, which passes upwards towards the surface, melting the overlying rock. The cold surface crust shrinks and cracks and the molten rock, or lava, pours forth, while parts of the crust may become pitched at an angle or drift apart. So it is that the planet's surface is formed partly by its own volcanic upheavals, and partly by bombardment from space.

What happens after that depends mainly on the planet's atmosphere. An airless world, with no wind and rain to crack and wear down the surface rocks, will see its cratered and cracked surface lie unchanged for thousands of millions of years, except for the occasional impact of a meteoroid and the steady descent of particles of meteoric dust. This is the state of Mercury and our Moon; in their harsh faces is written the chaotic early history of the Solar System.

Venus: the masked planet

About every nineteen months, a beautiful object appears in our evening skies. Brighter than any star, it hangs in the west like a distant lamp, catching the eye soon after the Sun has set. As dusk deepens its silvery light grows so bright that some people claim to have seen their own shadow cast by it. In an astronomical telescope, its beauty remains. Like Mercury, it is closer to the Sun than we are,

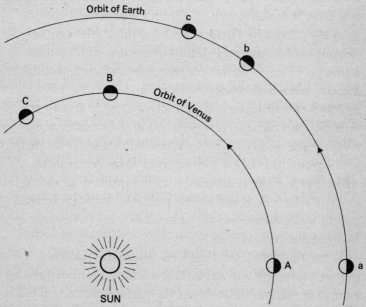

Figure 8 Venus takes about 56 days to travel through a quarter of its orbit around the Sun, but because the Earth is also moving it has to travel on to C – another 14 days or so – before it appears to have reached elongation

its average distance being 108 million kilometres, and it passes through phases, though more slowly because it takes 224 days to complete an orbit around the Sun.

But why does Venus seem to take nineteen months to go around the Sun, when its year is only 224 days? The reason is that the platform from which we view Venus – our Earth – is itself moving around the Sun, and we have to take our own motion into account. In *figure 7*, the explanation of the phases of Mercury assumes that the Earth is stationary. *Figure 8* shows how the motion of the Earth makes Venus appear to move more slowly. As an example, we start with Venus at inferior conjunction on the near side of the Sun, at A, moving out towards its elongation or half-phase position at B. It takes about fifty-six days to cover this quarter of its orbit, but during this time the Earth has moved from a to b, so that Venus does not yet appear to be at elongation. The two planets have to move on for two more weeks until, at C and c, Venus appears at its greatest distance from the Sun. This slowing effect happens throughout its orbit. The same is true for Mercury, but the difference between its real (88-day) and apparent (116-day) periods is much smaller, because Mercury moves so fast around the Sun that the Earth's motion can do little to slow it down!

Even a small telescope can show the phase of Venus. (Binoculars show it well during the crescent phase, near inferior conjunction, because it is then nearest to the Earth, as shown in *figure 9*.) But to see markings on the planet has been a frustrating job for astronomers for three and a half centuries. Venus owes its brilliance to its covering of cloud. As far as we know this cloud never clears, and all that observers can look for is vague

Figure 9 The small disc shows Venus near superior conjunction, when it is about 250 million kilometres away. When near inferior conjunction it shows as a large, thin crescent less than 50 million kilometres away

markings that might suggest the direction of the winds that blow these clouds across the surface. Until very recently there was no clue as to what the surface is like, and ideas of the length of its day varied from about twenty-four hours to as long as 224 days, the length of its year.

Astronomers poring over the tiny disc of Mercury used to think that its day was as long as its year. This would mean that the same part of its surface always faced the Sun, just as the Moon keeps its same side towards the Earth. But the truth about Venus is stranger still. About fifteen years ago, astronomers managed to send radio transmissions to Venus and receive back the feeble echo. Unlike light rays, radio waves can pass through clouds, and the reflection came back from the solid surface. By measuring the way the radio waves were altered by the reflection, the speed at which the surface rotates could be worked out. It came to 243 days, which is *longer* than the planet's year!

This is curious enough. But measures of the speed at which the clouds move, made partly by Earth-based observatories and also by the *Mariner 10* spacecraft in 1974, show that they are whirling round the planet in about four days. We do not know why they should move at this tremendous rate, but one thing is certain – there must be furious winds in the Venusian atmosphere, higher even than hurricane-force winds on the Earth. Although Venus is almost exactly the same size as the Earth (its diameter of 12,100 kilometres is only 650 kilometres smaller), it seems to be completely different.

We knew very little about conditions on the surface of Venus until Soviet space probes were sent there. Eight have so far landed between 1966 and 1975, and the two most recent, *Veneras 9* and *10*, sent back photographs of the surface in October 1975. These show a broken, rocky landscape. The temperature of the surface is about 480°C, and the pressure at the bottom of the atmosphere is about a hundred times that of the Earth's (the same as the pressure you would find at a depth of a thousand metres in the sea). It is not surprising that none of the spacecraft have survived for more than an hour after landing in such unearthly conditions. To make things still worse, many astronomers believe that this fuming, stifling atmosphere contains a good deal of sulphuric acid, which eats away most metals.

Most of the atmosphere of Venus is composed of the choking gas carbon dioxide, and this gives astronomers the problem of explaining why it should be so different from the Earth's atmosphere. After all, Venus is almost the same size as the Earth and is probably made up in a similar way. We do know (or at least we think it quite likely) that hundreds of millions of years ago, before life forms had properly developed, the Earth's atmosphere contained a good deal of carbon dioxide, mostly given out by volcanic activity. This gas was largely cleared away by the arrival of plants, which absorbed the carbon and released the oxygen into the atmosphere. On Venus, perhaps because it never grew cool enough, or because there was not enough water, plants never developed and the carbon dioxide remained. Not only that, it blanketed in the Sun's already fierce heat, making the surface grow still hotter and releasing more carbon dioxide from the boiling-hot rocks. Under its murky veil, the surface of Venus turned into a roasting, choking hell, a place to which no life ever came, a place that space travellers of the future, no matter how ambitious, will surely always avoid. Such must be the face behind the silvery, twinkling light of the evening star.

The Earth: our home

One of the most important results of the space age has been the photographs of the Earth taken from far out in space. They have made many people realize for the first time that the world we live on is a round ball flying through the void. Of course, everybody *knew* this because they had been told about it, but it took those photographs to show how small we are, how helpless – and how alone. Alongside these pictures we can now place close-up photographs of the planets Mercury, Venus, Mars and Jupiter, all taken from space, showing that our Earth is just one – neither the biggest nor the smallest – among the community of planets that circle the Sun.

We have already seen that the four inner planets, from Mercury to Mars, are completely different from the outer, gaseous planets. But there are huge differences amongst these inner worlds. Mercury and Venus are completely hostile to life as we know it and Mars, too, seems to be a cratered waste with only a very thin atmosphere. Our Earth is so startlingly different that it makes us blink. Over half of its surface is covered with water, something that is scarce or unknown on other planets. Its air contains oxygen, again rare or unknown (except in compounds with other elements) elsewhere. Water and oxygen, to us, are the stuff of life. Another important difference is temperature. The surfaces of Mercury and Mars change by hundreds of degrees between day and night, while Venus is so hot that living cells as we know them would be destroyed. The greatest range of temperature recorded on the Earth's surface, from poles to equator, is about 150°C, but the temperature at any one place changes by far less than this from summer to winter.

We can explain some, but not all, of these great differences from the other planets. For instance, why has Venus hardly any water or water vapour in its atmosphere, which is where it should be after boiling off the surface? We can explain the presence of oxygen on the Earth by the action of plants – but for the plants to start developing, conditions had to be right in the way of warmth and wetness. Of course, the temperature of the Earth was dependent on its distance from the Sun, once its own inner heat began to die down and the surface cooled to the point where life was possible.

If we moved the Earth towards the Sun until it was at the distance of Venus (108 million kilometres, instead of its present 150 million), temperatures everywhere would rise to near the boiling point of water. The water vapour would mix into the atmosphere, trapping the Sun's heat near the surface, and the temperature would shoot up still more until killing Venus-like conditions were everywhere. In fact, a movement towards the Sun of just a few million kilometres could have this effect and no life of our type would then be possible. On the other hand, a few million kilometres further away from the Sun and temperatures would drop so that nowhere did they rise much above the freezing-point of water. It would be a world of snow and ice, perhaps partly melting for a few weeks in midsummer, but intensely cold at night and during the gloomy winter. Plant activity would die off, and oxygen would steadily waste away without being replaced. The frozen oceans, which at the moment in their unfrozen state do so much to warm the air in regions such as the British Isles, would be vast refrigerators.

Another thought, too, must make us feel lucky to be

alive at all. We have seen that the Sun sends out rays of all types: some friendly and useful such as the light we see by and the heat rays that warm us, and others dangerous. Astronauts venturing into space must be careful to protect themselves from the lethal rays. The Earth's surface is safe because they are turned away by a layer of oxygen atoms high in the atmosphere that have had their atomic structure altered by the solar rays. This modified oxygen is called **ozone**. It is extraordinary to think that the Sun's energy has created an ozone barrier which protects us from the bad effects of its own radiation!

However, the situation is very finely balanced. If we were a little closer to the Sun, the increased radiation would be able to pass through the ozone, and living cells would be destroyed. Not much further away and the ozone would cut off some of the 'healthy' radiation which stimulates growth. Ozone is a very delicate substance, easily destroyed. It is no wonder that some scientists are worried about the effects of atmospheric pollution on this life-giving and life-saving layer.

So far we have looked at our planet from the point of view of the surface conditions. What of the solid globe? How does it compare with its fellow inner planets? The answer seems to be that there is not a great deal of difference. All the inner planets formed with iron and nickel cores, surrounded by a thick layer of hot or warm rock and covered with a cold, brittle crust that fractured easily. It is hard to see how there can be any great difference in the way they were formed. But both Mercury and Mars are much smaller than the Earth and must have cooled down more quickly, so that their surfaces are now rigid. This theory is backed up by the presence of ancient craters, particularly on Mercury. There may also be some low, weathered craters on Venus, but crater formations are certainly not obvious on the Earth's surface, although we do find very old ring-shaped structures, so weathered that only by high-altitude or satellite photography can their forms be well seen.

On the whole, though, the surface of the Earth was formed by its own internal activity, which covered up the impact craters that must have scarred its surface in the very early days. The crust fractured and slipped, producing mountain ranges where the sections came together and forced themselves up, and leaving huge basins (now seas) in the gaps. The Earth is still very hot inside and these movements in its crust, betrayed by earthquakes, still go on.

Ideas about the way life started on Earth, and the huge shifts of the continents on their molten-rock carpets, are fascinating, but we are looking at the Earth as a planet among its fellows. What really matters to us is that at some point in the remote past, about two thousand million years ago, conditions on its surface were right for primitive plants to start growing. Once the plants began to thrive and to pass oxygen into what then must have been a steamy, carbon dioxide atmosphere, the stage was set. Short of a calamity, such as the Sun surging up or dying down, or the surface of the planet becoming completely covered with water, this life would almost certainly develop and adapt. How the living cells came into being in the first place is a question that so far has not been answered.

The Moon: scarred and silent

To us, the Moon is the second most important body in the sky. But this is simply because it is so close to us. With a diameter of 3,476 kilometres, it is only the sixth largest satellite in the Solar System, three of Jupiter's family and one each of Saturn's and Neptune's moons being larger. Nobody could really say that the Moon counts for much in the astronomical scene.

But a nearby observer in space might have a different view. He would see the white and blue planet Earth, with its much smaller, crater-scarred moon circling it once in a month about 384,000 kilometres away. He would be struck by the complete difference between the two worlds – one airless and dead, its surface bare to the harshness of space, and the other clothed in air and clouds, washed by rain and lapped by the waters of its seas: a paradise!

He would also notice something else. Although the Moon is much smaller than some other satellites, it is still quite large compared with the planet to which it belongs. Its diameter is over a quarter of that of the Earth, which is big for a satellite. Many people think of the Earth and Moon as forming a kind of double planet, and it seems very likely that they were formed together when the solar nebula condensed. The gravity of the Earth would not have been strong enough to capture the Moon and pull it into orbit if the Moon had started life as a separate small planet circling the Sun.

Why, then, if they were formed from the same materials, are they so different? It is all a question of size. There is much more material in the Earth than in the Moon, and its interior could stay warm for longer, just as the embers of a big fire will stay warm long after a small fire has grown cold. During the bombardment of small bodies that caused most of the craters on the Moon and the inner planets about four thousand million years ago, the Earth's surface was still undergoing convulsions as its under layers heaved and burst through.

Nothing like this happened on the Moon. After the great crater-forming age, the surface stayed practically unchanged except for some huge flows of molten rock (lava) that spread and solidified darkly on the surface, forming the grey plains that make up the eyes and mouth of the Man in the Moon. Most astronomers believe that by three thousand million years ago, the Moon's crust had thickened and set hard, leaving the surface practically unchanged since that time. How else can we explain how the *Apollo 12* astronauts picked up a piece of rock from the surface that has turned out to be four and a half thousand million years old? If the Moon had continued in an active state, as the Earth has, such ancient fragments would have been covered up and lost. These very old lunar fragments must have been blasted out from below the surface by the impacts that formed the later craters, and have been lying there undisturbed ever since.

If the Moon had been larger it would also have held on to an atmosphere, because the extra pull of gravity would have stopped the bouncing atoms of gas from escaping into space. An atmosphere, even a thin one, might have made a big difference. Winds could have started to blow, and dust storms would have swept over the surface, wearing down the peaks of the mountains and craters. On Mars, which is twice the diameter of the Moon, this has happened. The Moon was just too small, and all its gases have leaked away.

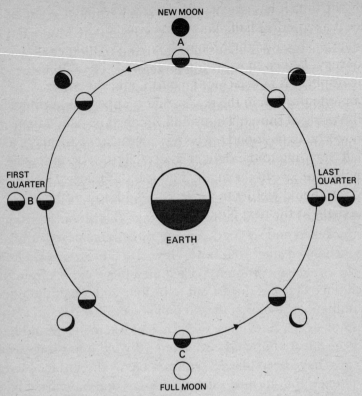

Figure 10 The phases of the Moon

How about the Moon as it appears in our sky? It passes through a cycle of phases in twenty-nine and a half days, and *figure 10* shows why. At position A it lies between the Earth and the Sun, and its night side is turned towards us. This is New Moon, and it cannot be seen at this time unless it chances to pass directly in front of the Sun, producing an eclipse as its black outline blocks out the solar disc. After New it moves to the left of the Sun and appears in the evening sky as a crescent. This crescent becomes wider as more of the sunlit hemisphere is seen.

By the time it has reached B, about a week after New, we see it as a perfect half. This phase is usually called First Quarter, because the Moon has covered a quarter of its journey. It then moves on to position C. The sunlit hemisphere is now facing the Earth, and the Moon is opposite the Sun in the sky, so that it appears as a round disc rising at sunset. This is Full Moon. The Moon then moves on to position D, where it once again appears as a half, standing to the right of the Sun in the sky and rising in the east late in the night. This is Last Quarter. The Moon then dwindles to a crescent and is lost in the daylight at the next New Moon.

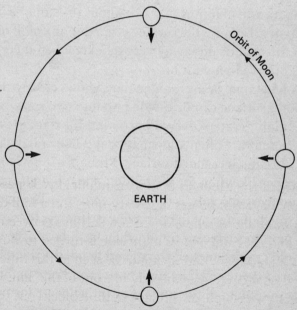

Figure 11 The Moon keeps the same face towards the Earth because it spins on its axis in the same time as it takes to travel round the Earth. In this diagram the 'bulge' on the Moon is very exaggerated!

The Moon keeps the same face towards the Earth, which means (*figure 11*) that it spins on its axis in the same time that it takes to go round the Earth. This has happened because of the pull of the Earth raising a slight bulge on one hemisphere (only a few kilometres high, but enough) and gripping on that bulge, slowing the Moon down from a fast rate of spin to its 'captured' turning. Since the Moon turns round only once a month, its day and night each last a fortnight, and with our telescopes we can watch the slow movement of the shadows as the Sun rises and sets in the bleak lunar sky. At noon, the surface temperature is higher than that of boiling water, but much cooler than on Mercury or Venus. The night temperature of minus 150°C is about the same as on Mercury, because the surface is open to the chill of space and the heat drains away very quickly when there is no atmosphere to hold it in.

A telescope, or even binoculars, shows clearly that the Moon's surface can be divided up into two sorts of area: the bright, crater-covered parts, and the dark grey lava plains that are often known as 'seas'. The crater-lands are the old, impact-ruined surface. Probably the whole Moon was once like that, for the hidden side, photographed now by many spacecraft, is crater-covered too. The grey plains are much flatter, with only a few craters on them. They tell us of more recent times, when fresh lava overwhelmed the old craters, melted them, and flooded millions of square kilometres. The fresh craters on these plains are the ones that best tell the story of how they were formed. For example, on the lava plain around the beautiful eighty-kilometre diameter crater Copernicus, in the Ocean of Storms (see *figure 32*), we find multitudes of pock-marks a few kilometres across, where fragments from the impact were scattered. Apollo astronauts were able to pick up many fragments lying on the surface that must have come from deep layers thrown up in these explosions.

One of the biggest scars on the Moon does not show properly from the Earth because it lies at the western limb, and we did not know much about it until the *Orbiter* photographs were examined. This, the Mare Orientale, is about a thousand kilometres across, large enough to contain much of the British Isles! It was possibly formed by the collision of an unusually large body, perhaps 100 kilometres across, which blasted out a crater many times its own size and cracked the surrounding crust enough for it to collapse. Mare Orientale, like many features of the Moon, is scarred by later craters, but its huge rings can still be seen clearly.

Now, the Moon sleeps. Perhaps slight changes still occur on its surface: a rock may be dislodged as it expands and contracts in the heat, or a surface crack may widen slightly. But the sensitive measuring instruments left on the surface suggest that little is happening. On the Earth, with its ocean tides and almost continuous tremblings of the crust, they would record mad activity. Our Moon, once the scene of boiling tumult, now changes only with the slowly-moving shadows that creep over its scarred and silent face.

Mars: dying, dead, or dormant?

The history of our knowledge of Mars shows a great many ups and downs. In the last one and a half centuries, expert observers have formed all sorts of ideas about this fascinating

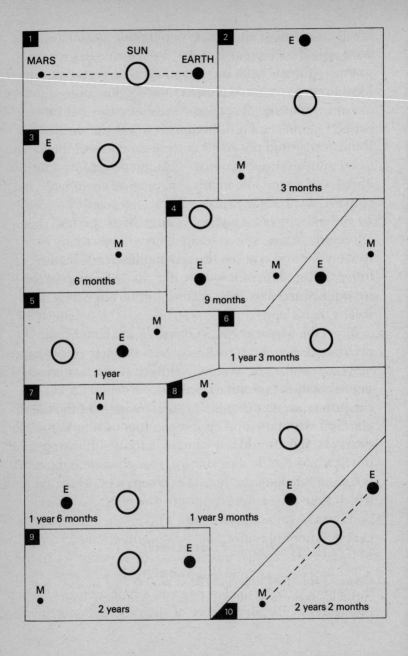

world, and almost all of them – including some dating from after the first space probes there – have been wrong.

The red world of Mars passes into good view from the Earth only every 780 days or so – about two years and two months. No other planet hides itself away for such a long period. Neither can it ever appear as large as the planets Venus and Jupiter; its 6,787 kilometre diameter globe can never appear larger than a ten millimetre disc seen from a distance of eighty-two metres. For most of the time, it is only about a third of this size. No wonder that astronomers have had difficulty in making up their minds about this planet!

Mars is the first of the planets that are further away from the Sun than our own world – its average distance from the Sun is about 228 million kilometres – and this means that it appears to pass right round the sky instead of just staying near the Sun. *Figure 12* shows how the two planets move around the Sun, and how Mars seems to move across the sky. We start with Mars on the opposite side of the Sun to the Earth, a position that is known as **conjunction**. At this time, Mars is invisible in the solar glare. As the planets proceed along their orbits, the Earth starts chasing after Mars, which swings out to the right of the Sun and can be seen rising in the east before dawn. It takes the Earth over a year to catch up with Mars, by which time the planet is opposite the Sun in our skies, a position known as **opposition**. This is when Mars is at its closest. After opposition, the Earth runs on ahead and Mars recedes rapidly, moving into the evening sky to the

Figure 12 How the Earth chases Mars around the Sun. Mars is at opposition between positions 5 and 6, just over a year after conjunction

left of the Sun and finally vanishing into its rays at the next conjunction.

The diagram tells us various things, good and bad, about our view of Mars. A good thing is that it does not pass through the phases that make observation of Mercury and Venus so difficult (it sometimes shows a slight phase, like the Moon about three days from full, but never enough to be a problem). A bad thing is that its distance from the Earth changes so much that we have a good view only for a few weeks around the time of opposition, which happens every other year.

A final point to make before turning to the planet itself is that the orbit is eccentric enough to matter. The distance of Mars from the Sun varies from 207 to 249 million kilometres. If an opposition happens when Mars is closest to the Sun (perihelion), it is many millions of kilometres closer to the Earth than at a distant opposition (aphelion). So some oppositions, such as the ones of 1956 and 1971, have been more useful to astronomers than others.

What have we found out about Mars, despite all these difficulties?

First of all, we are seeing a solid surface. The markings are so clear that astronomers two centuries ago could time the planet's spin to within a few seconds. Its day is equal to 24 hours 37 minutes 23 seconds, not much longer than our own. But on just about every other count, astronomers up to the present century have been wrong. The dark markings, which we now know are dusty plains, were once thought to be seas; later, many people saw them as huge areas of vegetation. Some Mars enthusiasts even imagined that the planet might have intelligent people living on it, and they drew markings that looked like narrow waterways to bring water from the thin polar caps to the 'deserts'. Even today, people well remember the time when Mars was supposed to have canals on it.

Before the space age, astronomers knew perfectly well that the atmosphere of Mars is much thinner than that of the Earth because of the clearness with which the surface markings usually show. But there must be air of some sort because quite regularly the surface dust is whipped up into tremendous clouds that cover the well-known features for several weeks. So there must be winds. But what is the surface of Mars really like? Nobody could know for certain, because the best telescopes on Earth could not show markings smaller than about 50 or 100 kilometres across.

In August 1965, the US spacecraft *Mariner 4* raced past Mars at a speed of about ten kilometres a second. The cameras on board had time to take and transmit twenty-two pictures of a small part of the surface. These, to everyone's surprise, showed craters like those on the Moon but much worn down, apparently from the battering by wind-borne dust. Two further probes in 1969, *Mariners 6* and 7, sent back clearer pictures, but told the same story. It looked as if the surface of Mars was a medley of ancient scars formed by bodies striking it thousands of millions of years ago, and about as dead as that of the Moon. Some people thought it pointless investigating further with more expensive spacecraft.

Fortunately, not everyone agreed. In November 1971, *Mariner 9* took its cameras into orbit around Mars. This meant that its view was not just of a small part of the surface, the sort that the other probes had sent back as they shot past. *Mariner 9* stayed in orbit and sent back over seven thousand pictures, in close-up, of the Martian surface, showing details just a few hundred metres across. Astronomers now found that the earlier probes had, unluckily, photographed very uninteresting regions of the planet. Certainly there were many old impact craters, but there was much more besides. They found huge volcanoes, regions where molten rock had been forced to the surface from beneath the crust. The largest, known as Olympus Mons (Mount Olympus), is about 600 kilometres across and twenty-five kilometres high, which is two and a half times the height of Everest! They found colossal valleys or canyons many times the size and depth of the Grand Canyon in Arizona. There are tremendous cliffs, formed by sections of the ground subsiding. All this shows that in the past the surface of Mars was moulding itself as well as receiving the cratering blows of interplanetary particles. Neither the Moon nor Mercury shows much evidence of this – but the Earth does. Perhaps, before our great oceans had formed and the wind and rain had started to wear down the surface, the Earth looked something like Mars does today?

What excited investigators more than anything else was the discovery of what look like ancient river-beds. We know for certain that today there are no lakes or seas on Mars. Certainly the polar caps contain frozen water, but in the summer they seem to melt away without flooding the surrounding surface, so there cannot be a great deal of it. And although thin white clouds sometimes float over the surface, it seems unlikely that it ever rains on Mars. If there is a lot of hidden water, it must be frozen permanently beneath the surface of the planet, where the temperature never rises above the freezing point. But these channels certainly look as if they were formed by running water. Some look ancient and worn, while others look quite new. It is possible that they are washed out every few centuries, or even every few thousand years, by a wet season, although nobody has explained why such wet seasons should occur. But how else do we explain these channels?

Eighty years or so ago, practically everybody was prepared to believe in Martians. Astronomers thought that the planet was warm enough, and the atmosphere dense enough, for intelligent beings to live on it. In 1938, a too-realistic broadcast sent thousands of people in the USA into a panic, thinking that a story about Martians landing on the Earth was the real thing! We have other ideas now. The air is very thin (about one hundred times thinner than our own), and anyway is made up mostly of unbreathable carbon dioxide. At Martian noon, near the equator, the air temperature rises to minus 30°C, but at night it drops to minus 80°C, and is much lower near the poles. Most of the time, then, the temperature is bitterly cold. But it is still just possible that some very simple organisms could survive. One of the hopes of the two *Viking* probes that made a rendezvous with the planet in 1976 was to test for these.

Mars has two tiny moons, called Phobos and Deimos. The *Mariner* cameras photographed them as irregular chunks of rock just a few dozen kilometres across, pitted with craters from old impacts. Perhaps they were once free roaming bodies, captured by the gravitational pull of Mars. But they will be of little use in lightening the bitter, windswept nights of this dead or dying world.

Jupiter: the star that failed?

Mighty above all other bodies in the Solar System after the Sun itself, Jupiter is in a class of its own. It would take 1300 bodies the size of the Earth to fill it, for its diameter is 142,800 kilometres. In fact, *all* the other planets in the Solar System could be crammed beneath its surface!

Jupiter is the first of the four remote worlds that we call the giant planets. On our journey outwards from the Sun we have passed the rocky inner planets. Then comes a huge gap of over 500 million kilometres. Thousands of tiny minor planets, known as **asteroids**, circle in this void. Beyond, influencing by its gravity everything that moves in the Solar System, Jupiter circles the Sun once in nearly twelve years at a distance of 778 million kilometres.

Jupiter and its mighty fellows in no way resemble the inner planets. They have no rocky surface crusts in which to find written the ancient records of impacts, lava flows and volcanic peaks, valleys and canyons formed by collapse. Instead, they are globes of gas, liquid, and ice – mostly hydrogen. The 'surfaces' that astronomers observe are only the outer layers, in which compounds of hydrogen with other elements, such as nitrogen and carbon, form tinted markings. A landing on any of these planets would be impossible because the craft would be pulled into them until the pressure made them collapse.

Although it is at such a great distance from the Earth, Jupiter is so huge that we enjoy a better view of it than we have of any other planet. (Venus sometimes appears larger, but only when it is a thin crescent.) Jupiter comes to opposition every thirteen months or so, because the Earth has to travel only slightly more than once round the Sun to catch up with it again (*figure 13*). Its sunlit face is

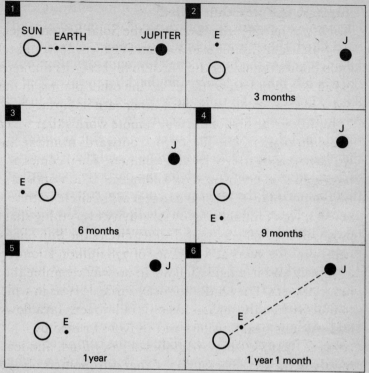

Figure 13 Jupiter moves round the Sun much more slowly than does the Earth. After our planet has made a complete orbit, in one year, it has to travel on for only a month to catch up with Jupiter again

always turned towards us. At opposition it looks about as large as a disc ten millimetres in diameter seen from forty-four metres away. This means that even binoculars can show it looking larger than a star, and they will also reveal the four largest of its family of fourteen known moons.

Even a small astronomical telescope shows that Jupiter is not perfectly round. It is flattened at the poles, and this tells us that it must be spinning quickly. What happens is

65

that the material near the equator is flung outwards by an effect known as **centrifugal force**. Even our small and solid Earth shows a small flattening, about forty kilometres. But the huge planet Jupiter is spinning round once in less than ten hours, and the difference is about 8,800 kilometres. To time the length of its day accurately, recognizable markings in the cloud belts are followed and timed until they are carried back to the same position by the planet's spin. When this is done – and there is plenty of detail lasting long enough for the purpose – we find that the parts of the atmosphere near the equator rotate once in 9 hours $50\frac{1}{2}$ minutes, while the rest of the planet takes a little longer (9 hours 56 minutes). This difference proves that the surface of Jupiter cannot be a solid one.

The markings on Jupiter are so easy to see that they have been observed for hundreds of years. Jupiter is certainly the best-observed planet in the Solar System, and the photographs taken by *Pioneer 10* in 1973 and *Pioneer 11* in 1974 have not produced the complete surprises that the Mars pictures did. Most of the markings last only a few weeks or months before they lose their form or vanish, and they are probably formed by the circulation of different tinted materials in the surface layers. There is some evidence that this material is rising to the surface in the light zones, and falling back beneath it in the dark belts. These zones and belts keep more or less the same position on the planet's surface, and they have been given names (*figure 14*). Such belts as the North and South Equatorial Belts can be seen with a very small astronomical telescope, although the detail seen through them becomes more complicated as the telescope grows larger.

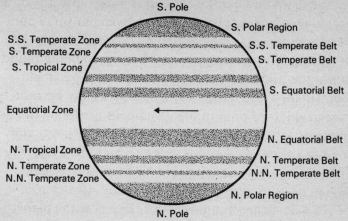

Figure 14 The positions of the dark belts and light zones commonly seen on the planet Jupiter. The drawing has south at the top because astronomical telescopes usually turn the view upside-down

Some features on Jupiter, however, seem to be much longer-lasting than others. A number of light-coloured spots a few thousand kilometres across have been followed for years, while the famous Great Red Spot, a huge oval marking up to 40,000 kilometres long and about 14,000 kilometres wide (large enough to contain about three Earths!), was first seen soon after the invention of the telescope. Sometimes it fades and sometimes, as in 1975, it is a striking reddish-pink. Nobody has yet come up with a good explanation for the Red Spot and its fellows, but we do know that they drift about a good deal in the surface slush of ice and ammonia crystals (smelling-salts), as well as helium and methane. Methane is the pungent gas that occurs on our planet over swamps as vegetable and animal matter rots away. This unpleasant mixture would make Jupiter and the other giant planets very unwelcoming worlds, particularly at their temperatures of around 200°C below zero!

We might expect Jupiter to have captured a great many moons in its time, but the four bright ones – Io, Europa, Ganymede and Callisto – were probably formed at the same time as the planet. Of the four, probably only Europa is smaller than the Moon, and they all seem to keep the same face turned towards Jupiter. They form a pretty sight through a small telescope, but the other ten known moons are too tiny to be detected except with giant instruments.

We have called Jupiter the star that failed. There is a good reason for this. In Chapter 2 it was mentioned that the Sun must have been formed when a huge cloud – consisting, as everything in the universe does, mostly of hydrogen – collapsed and grew hot enough for nuclear reactions to begin. At the same time, or slightly later, the planets condensed from the same sort of material. The inner planets were too small to hold on to the dancing hydrogen, or perhaps most of the hydrogen near the Sun had been picked up by this star anyway. But mighty Jupiter pulled in hydrogen and everything else, just as the young Sun had done. The difference was that Jupiter was not quite big enough. The bigger the cloud, the hotter it will become as it contracts. The interior of Jupiter is certainly hot – probably about 30,000°C – but it never reached the temperature at which hydrogen atoms start to change their structure and turn into helium.

It may have been a near thing. Some stars that we observe have much less material in them than the Sun – less than a tenth, perhaps even as little as a hundredth. Jupiter has about a thousandth of the Sun's material. If the solar nebula had been thicker, Jupiter would have grown so large that it might have eaten up the material for the other young planets as well. Its furnaces would have started, and a star would have been born. The Sun would have a companion – but we should not have been here to see it.

Saturn: the ringed planet

If it were not for one thing, Saturn would be looked upon as a junior and unexciting brother of its neighbour Jupiter. It is still a huge world, 120,000 kilometres across, with a volume of about 750 Earths. But its cloudy surface shows very little in the way of markings, even when seen through the large telescopes necessary for a good view.

Although no probe has yet visited Saturn to take close-up views and measurements, we suspect that it must be made up in much the same way as Jupiter. But for some reason it is much less dense. The density of a body tells us how much material there is in a certain volume of it. If we took an average sample of the Earth measuring a centimetre along each side (about as big as a small sugar cube), it would weigh about five and a half grams. If we took a similar average sample of the giant planets Jupiter, Uranus or Neptune, it would weigh about one and a half grams because of all the light hydrogen and other substances that are present. But a sample of Saturn would weigh only three-quarters of a gram. Since water would weigh just one gram, we can enjoy the fantastic image of Saturn floating about in some stupendous ocean! Saturn spins on its axis in about ten and a quarter hours, and its low density means that it is even more flattened at the poles than Jupiter.

A strange world, indeed, moving around the Sun in its twenty-nine-and-a-half-year orbit at a distance of 1,427 million kilometres, masked by its pungent gas-clouds. Saturn shines in our skies with a yellowish light, bright enough to be found easily, but nothing like the white, brilliant planet Jupiter. The ancient astronomers, with nothing better than the naked eye to inform them, called the planet after the mythical god of time, a thoroughly unpleasant being who destroyed his male children in case one of them should become his rival – and the one who escaped, Jupiter, did just that.

With an astronomical telescope, however, there is no rival to Saturn. Floating in the field of view we see a miraculous sight: a world surrounded by a shining ring. (A diagram of the ring system is shown in *figure 15*.) In fact, our eyes are not on the planet at all but on this unbelievable halo.

What happened in the distant past of the Solar System's history, we can only guess. Perhaps a young, close moon of Saturn came so close to the planet that its fierce pull tore the body apart. We know that such a thing *could* happen. Perhaps more likely is that some of the clouds of small particles, which later condensed into Saturn's family of ten moons, became spread out around the planet. As millions of years passed they would all have been forced into a thin sheet because this is the form in which the pull of Saturn would least disturb them. Then, in this sheet, other forces would have arranged them into three main rings, one inside the other, no doubt with other particles scattered elsewhere. From our great distance the rings look solid, but they are really made up of countless icy particles probably just a few centimetres across. Ice reflects light well, and the rings of Saturn reflect the dim sunlight much better than do the planet's cloud tops.

The scale and thinness of the rings takes everyone by surprise. Across their outer edge they measure about 270,000 kilometres, or twenty-one times the diameter of the Earth; but they are too thin to measure properly at all. Every fifteen years or so they appear edge-on to observers on the Earth, and when this happens they disappear from view altogether. All we can do is say that they must be no more than twenty kilometres thick. Even with this upper limit, a scale model of the rings the diameter of a dinner plate would have a thickness not much more than one ten-thousandth of a millimetre!

Even a small astronomical telescope shows a black line running round the ring. This is a gap, known as Cassini's division, 2,700 kilometres wide. Particles have been forced out of this division by the regular gravitational action of Saturn's moons. There are other, much fainter, divisions as well. Inside rings A and B (*figure 15*), which are separated

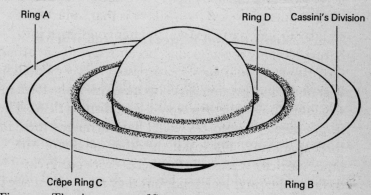

Figure 15 The ring system of Saturn

by Cassini's division, is the faint ring C, known as the Crêpe ring. Probably the particles in this ring are thinly scattered and reflect much less sunlight. A fourth ring, D, lies very close to the planet's equator and has been seen by few people.

Saturn's family of moons extends to ten. The closest, Janus, is only 26,000 kilometres beyond the outermost ring, and whirls round Saturn in eighteen hours. The furthest out, Phoebe, is at the huge distance of thirteen million kilometres, with an orbit period of 550 days. Both of these are tiny bodies just a few hundred kilometres across. Others are larger, and the biggest of all, Titan, may be the largest satellite in the Solar System; it is certainly larger than the planet Mercury, and seems to have a cloudy atmosphere of hydrogen and methane. But when we think of Saturn, we think of the rings: the wonder of the Solar System. Is it surprising that amateur astronomers turn their telescopes again and again to this miracle in the skies? Everyone is looking forward to September 1979, when *Pioneer 11* is due to send back the first close-up photographs of this amazing world.

Uranus, Neptune and Pluto: forgotten worlds

The planets we have surveyed so far had been recognized by their movement around the sky thousands of years ago. Astronomers right up to the 18th century had no reason to suppose that any more remained to be found. But in 1781 an amateur astronomer, William Herschel, discovered a new, distant planet during a survey of the sky. Known as Uranus, this world brought fame to Herschel and doubled the known diameter of the Solar System. With a diameter four times that of the Earth, Uranus is a substantial world, and it has five satellites. But at a distance of 2,870 million kilometres, it appears so faint that it can only just be seen with the naked eye. The year of Uranus is equal to eighty-four of our years, so that it has gone round the Sun only two and a half times since its discovery.

Remoter worlds circle beyond, but the scene from Uranus would be very gloomy, supposing that we could see anything through the hydrogen and methane clouds. The Sun would be a faraway pinpoint, like an intensely brilliant star, no more; full daylight would be duller than the most overcast day on Earth. Looking towards the Sun, the planet Saturn would swing slowly out and back again as a morning or evening object, a complete cycle taking forty-five years. It would never appear much further away from the Sun than the planet Mercury does to us, while Jupiter would be much closer in, and a difficult naked-eye object. The inner planets might not be visible at all. Uranus's outer companion, Neptune, would shine dimly at opposition every 160 years or so. Our visit would only serve to remind us that the Earth is a good place on which to live!

The day on Uranus lasts for about eleven hours, so that it is another fast spinner, although its tiny disc shows very little in the way of markings. But something else about its rotation makes it unique. All the other planets stand almost upright in their orbits as they spin on their axes, so that day and night follow a normal course. The axis of Uranus, however, is lying down on its side (*figure 16*). This means that each pole is in continuous sunlight for half of its 84-year period. Try to imagine if life would be possible on our planet if large parts of each hemisphere were in

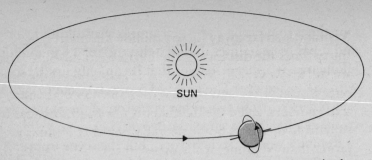

Figure 16 The axis of the planet Uranus is tilted over almost in the plane of its orbit around the Sun

continuous daylight or night for up to six months at a time.

Uranus was found by chance. Half a century later it caused mathematicians concern and astronomers despair. The movement of a planet around the Sun is controlled by gravity, not just the pull of the Sun itself (though that is much the most important) but also the much weaker pulls of the other planets, particularly Jupiter. Once astronomers had placed Uranus accurately, it should have been possible to predict for many years ahead just where in the sky it would lie. But Uranus started 'wandering'. These effects were not large by ordinary standards, and astronomers only began to worry when the error was about equal to the thickness of a human hair seen from a distance of a metre or so. Two mathematicians came up with the answer. There had to be another, unknown planet beyond Uranus, which was pulling it out of position. The position of this new planet in the sky was calculated, and in 1846 it was found. The discovery of Neptune, as the planet was called, caused a sensation, since most of the work had been done at the desk rather than at the telescope!

Neptune is so far away (4,497 million kilometres, or thirty times the distance of the Earth from the Sun), that we still know very little about it. It goes around the Sun once in 165 years, and the length of the day is about sixteen hours. Even the diameter is uncertain because it is so hard to measure. Some people think that Uranus is larger than Neptune, while others think the opposite; the safest thing is to put them both at about 50,000 kilometres. In the scale model on page 13, with the Sun ten centimetres across, they are represented by apple pips at distances of 206 and 323 metres. Neptune has two satellites and one of them, Triton, may be as large as Saturn's Titan.

Pluto, the outermost known planet, is another world of mystery. It is much smaller than the giant planets and may be the smallest planet after Mercury, with a diameter of about 6,000 kilometres. Found in 1930, a medium-sized astronomical telescope is needed to view it. Careful observations of its brightness show a regular change in about six days nine hours, and this seems to be the length of its day, the changes in brightness probably being caused by light and dark patches on its surface. Some recent observations suggest that this surface is coated with a layer of methane gas, frozen by the bitter chill of about 230°C below zero.

One very strange thing about Pluto is the eccentricity of its orbit, which will carry it closer to the Sun than Neptune between 1979 and 1999. After that it will swing away on its lonely 248-year circuit, and the year 2113 will find it furthest away, at aphelion, 7,375 million kilometres from the Sun or fifty times the distance of the Earth from the Sun. This tiny world marks the border of interstellar space.

5 The minor planets, meteors and comets

The planets that revolve around the Sun, and the satellites that revolve around many of the planets, seem to have all been formed from the huge cloud, the solar nebula, that spread in a thin disc around the Sun either at the time of our star's birth or very soon afterwards. The question of where the nebula came from will be asked, and partly answered, later. The other question is what happened to the part of the nebula that did not condense into the planets and satellites that we find in the sky? There was probably enough to make dozens of sets of planets!

The short answer is that we don't know what happened to most of it. It probably fell into the Sun, though some may have been forced out into space by the Sun's increased radiation when it came up to full power. There is certainly no sign of these huge amounts of planet-forming material now. But, scattered through the Solar

System and the near surroundings of space, we find odd specks of solid matter that can only be what is left over from those exciting days.

The first clue that the major planets are not the only solid bodies in the Solar System came on the first day of the 19th century (1 January 1801), when an Italian astronomer discovered a tiny world moving around the Sun between the orbits of Mars and Jupiter. Astronomers before him had noted the huge gap between these planets, and wondered if anything filled it. This minute world only a few hundred kilometres across was the first of a whole assortment of 'flying rocks', now known to number several thousand, that have been found in this zone of the Solar System. We call them the minor planets to distinguish them from the nine major planets that have already been described. Most are just a few kilometres across. Probably there are countless thousands smaller than this, but they are too faint for astronomers to pick up unless their orbits happen to carry them close to the Earth.

If we assembled all the minor planets known, and those swarms of others assumed to exist, we should not produce much of a planet. It would be much smaller than any of the major planets. So, unless some ancient, unstable world literally blew up soon after the Solar System was formed and threw most of its material out into interstellar space (and that would require some explaining!), these fragments must be parts of the solar nebula that condensed so far, but never made a planet of respectable size and were never swept up by any of the other planets. This is what most astronomers believe today. For some reason, the proto-planet formed between Mars and Jupiter never became big enough to attract really large amounts of material. It paid the penalty. Collisions with other rocky bodies broke down the larger planets, and the smaller ones whirled on. If Jupiter is a star which failed, the minor planets are certainly a failed world.

The minor planets which approach the Earth are the remains of what must once have been a forbidding army of missiles flying around the Solar System. The craters on Mercury, the Moon and Mars tell us that; the rocky bodies flew apparently where they wished, and created havoc on the surfaces of these forming worlds. Now, most of them keep to the zone where they were formed; the roving ones, those with orbits that brought them into the regions of the inner planets, are nearly all destroyed. But some remain, and *figure 17* shows the orbits of several that have been observed. Because their orbits pass near that of the Earth, some have become known by the rather dramatic name of 'Earth-grazers'.

This does not, of course, mean that they are literally shooting right past the Earth's surface. It is just that astronomers become excited if anything, apart from the Moon, passes within a few million kilometres of our planet! The closest known approach of a minor planet to the Earth happened in the winter of 1937–38, when a tiny world about two kilometres across, known as Hermes, passed the Earth at about twice the distance of the Moon. Some of these adventurous bodies swing in too close to the Sun for their own comfort – take unhappy Icarus, for instance, which passes inside the orbit of Mercury at perihelion and beyond the orbit of Mars at aphelion.

Now a body such as Hermes, although very small compared with almost everything else known in the Solar System, is still very large by human standards. If it did hit

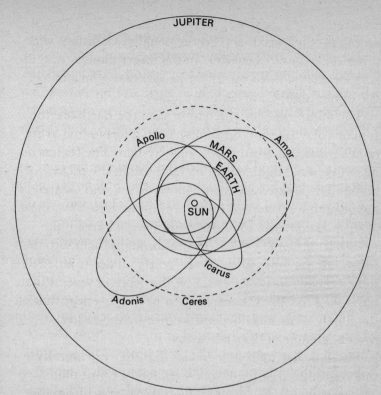

Figure 17 The orbits of most minor planets lie near the path of Ceres (shown as a dotted line). This drawing shows the orbits of some unusual minor planets. The orbits of the Earth, Mars and Jupiter are shown to scale

the Earth it would form a crater large enough to wipe out a city. What of all the other interplanetary particles, much smaller than this, which we could never hope to see with the most powerful telescope? There must be hundreds or thousands more down to a few metres across, and many, many smaller again than this. In fact, millions of particles collide with the Earth every day. Most are tiny, microscopic grains which are halted while they are passing through the atmosphere because they have so little energy, and float down to the ground. Objects the size of a small coin are much rarer and leave a streak of luminous, heated gases behind them as they plunge through the air at speeds of many kilometres a second. The tremendous heat destroys them at once, and they are crumbling into fine dust at the very moment when somebody on the Earth's surface looks up at the meteor or shooting star that has caught their eye. Still larger bodies weighing several kilograms, will leave a brilliant streak, and they may not be completely burned up before landing as a **meteorite**. Strangely enough, meteorites land quite gently. Although they come into the atmosphere at tremendous speed, they lose almost all of it before touching ground and drop no faster than a thrown stone.

These days, meteorites are considered really interesting. If the planets were all formed at the same time, the materials that went to make them must be of the same age. But the only planets that we have so far sampled – the Earth and the Moon – can only offer us rocks from near the surface. These rocks have already gone through intense heating and cooling. But minor planets and meteoroids probably never went through such fierce heating in the first place, because they did not grow large enough. Meteorites offer us the best fragments of early or primitive Solar System material – the best key to an understanding of how the planets were formed. This work is complicated and still in its early stages, but experimenters have already found evidence that the Sun and planets might have been formed from the material blasted out by an exploding star or **supernova**. We shall have more to say about this in Chapter 7.

There have been very few really big meteorite falls in recorded history. The largest was in Siberia in 1908, the blast flattening pine trees for about forty kilometres round about, and breaking windows up to eighty kilometres away! Unfortunately for scientists (but very luckily for everyone else) it fell into a remote, marshy region, and when the site was visited some years later the remains of the body had mostly disappeared.

Minor planets and large meteoroids seem to go around the Sun in their own lonely way. Even in the densest part

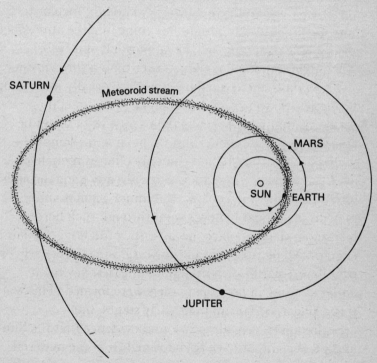

Figure 18 A meteor shower is seen when the Earth passes through a swarm of meteoroid particles

of the minor planet zone, they will probably be many thousands of kilometres apart. But the small objects that we see streaking through the atmosphere as meteors are different, for many of them move around the Sun in swarms. If the orbit of a swarm passes near the Earth's orbit, we shall then enjoy a shower of meteors while the Earth passes through the swarm (*figure 18*). Very often the meteoroids are sprinkled all along the orbit rather than bunched together, giving a shower at the same time every year when the Earth returns to the same place. There are about a dozen fairly strong meteor showers in the year, and many more feeble ones, while new showers appear from time to time.

Even in a shower, there are many kilometres between each meteoroid. So, while there may be millions pouring into the atmosphere, the part that one observer can see overhead will show far fewer than this. A rate of sixty meteors an hour is good, and only about three of the regular yearly showers are ever as lively as this. Sometimes, however, the Earth passes through such a dense swarm that the rate rises to hundreds an hour. In 1966, observers in the United States recorded *thousands* of meteors when the Earth passed through a very thick swarm on the fantastic night of 17 November.

If we sit and observe during a meteor shower, the tracks of the meteors all seem to come from a certain place amongst the stars. This is because they are all moving through space in the same direction. In *figure 19* we imagine that the observer sees some meteors flying down through the atmosphere. They are really keeping the same distance from each other, but to him they appear to be moving apart. If we stand in the middle of a long,

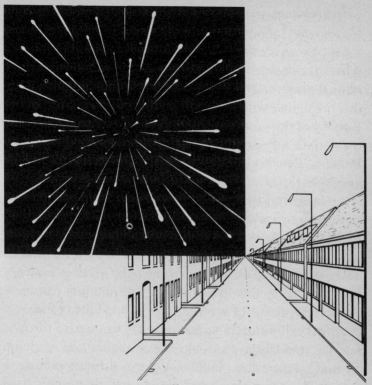

Figure 19 The meteors in a shower appear to radiate from a small region of the sky, even though they are really moving in parallel paths

straight street and look into the distance, the pavements and buildings seem to shrink together in the same way. This is the effect of perspective, which is such a common illusion in everyday life that we take no notice of it. The same thing is happening with meteors while they tear down through the high atmosphere at heights of about 200 kilometres down to fifty kilometres, but we usually see only the last few kilometres of their path, when they have brightened enough to be visible. This means that the observer sees a number of fairly short streaks, which he must plot on a star chart and back-track so as to find where they come together. Usually, meteor showers are named after the group of stars or constellation in which this point, or **radiant**, appears to lie. One of the strongest showers of the year, on 12 August, has its radiant in the constellation Perseus, and the meteors are known as the Perseids. By working out the path of a meteor through the atmosphere, its orbit around the Sun can be calculated.

To finish our survey of the Sun's family, we come to the most mysterious and spectacular bodies of all: the comets. Although we know something about what comets are, we have practically no idea at all of how they were formed. The main part of a comet is its nucleus, a rocky body or perhaps a collection of bodies just a few kilometres across. For some reason, the rock contains a good deal of what scientists call **volatile substances** (such as water frozen into ice, and frozen gases like the ammonia and methane we find on the outer planets). Volatile substances turn very easily into a gas when heated.

The second feature of a comet is its orbit, which is nearly always very elongated indeed, completely unlike any planet's orbit. The aphelion of most comets is beyond the orbit of Pluto, although some go no further from the Sun than the distance of Jupiter. At perihelion, however, they are nearly always within the Earth's orbit, and possibly even closer to the Sun than baking Mercury.

So a comet, during its revolution, undergoes a tremendous temperature change. It passes most of its life near aphelion, because its orbital speed is lowest when far from the Sun, and in the intense cold of minus 200°C or

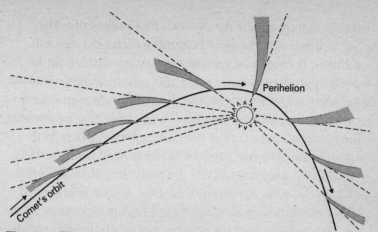

Figure 20 The main tail of a comet always points away from the Sun

less, everything is frozen and dead. But as it approaches the Sun, and the temperature rises, a cloud of warmed gas begins to develop. If it passes close to the Sun, this gas is poured off into space at a furious rate, together with countless particles of solid matter or dust. The force of the solar wind, combined with the tremendous speed of the comet, which can approach 100 kilometres a second if it passes really close to the Sun, combs these huge volumes of gas and dust back into the sensational tails that make bright comets so memorable (*figure 20*).

'Huge' is the word. Some of these tails may be millions of kilometres long. How can this be, when the body that produces them is only a few kilometres across? The answer is that the particles of dust, and the atoms of gas, are very, very thinly spread. A sample of a comet's tail would be millions of times thinner than a sample of our own air, but it is noticeable because interplanetary space is thinner still.

The comets which become famous grow tails. There

was a superb one in April 1976, and another in March 1970. But dozens of other comets pass round the Sun unnoticed except by astronomers. They have little or nothing in the way of a tail – just a hazy **coma**, or head. Perhaps they do not grow a tail because they never move close enough to the Sun to become really hot; or perhaps they are old comets that have been round again and again, and have lost most of their tail-making materials. Eventually all comets must die, and only their nucleus will remain. We know too that they scatter many solid particles of matter along their orbits, because some of the meteor showers that we see every year are travelling along the orbits of comets.

Most comets can be made out only when they are passing near the Sun and the Earth. *Figure 21* shows the orbit of the most famous comet of all, Halley's Comet, which was last seen when it swung past the Sun in 1910. We know its path very accurately and astronomers can pinpoint exactly where it is in the sky, but because it is still about as far away as Uranus no telescope in the world can detect it. Not until it has reached the orbit of Jupiter,

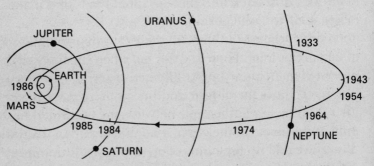

Figure 21 The orbit of Halley's comet, and the positions it will pass during its next return to the Sun

less than a year before it next sweeps around the Sun in 1986, are we likely to hear that it has been detected. So even known comets like this one are invisible for most of the time, while new comets come as a complete surprise. Every year, several new comets are discovered as they enter the Sun's region. Most are faint and stay that way, but sometimes bright comets, with fine tails, are suddenly spotted after creeping up to the Sun unobserved.

After watching the movement of a comet for several weeks, mathematicians can work out its orbit around the Sun. The shortest 'year' of any comet is three years and four months, but this is exceptional. About a hundred are known with periods of between six and eight years, which means that they reach the distance of Jupiter at aphelion. Most, however (and about 400 are now known) pass out to the realms of the outer planets or beyond. For instance, the splendid comet of 1976, Comet West (named after its discoverer, Richard West), which shone in the sky while this book was being written, will recede so far beyond the orbit of Pluto that it will not return for a million years!

Probably about half the comets that have been observed have orbits like that of Comet West. For incredible lengths of time they move slowly through remote regions of space that are not interplanetary, but interstellar. At these huge distances, perhaps a hundred thousand times the distance of the Earth from the Sun, there can be little difference between the brightness of the Sun and of some of the other stars that crowd in the dark sky. If we add up the number of comets with these huge orbits that have been observed in astronomy's history, and allow for the tremendous time that passes between each visit to the Sun, we find that there must be hundreds of thousands of these dark, frozen bodies, so far from the Sun that the pull of gravity can scarcely bind them at all.

Perhaps they are a part of the solar nebula that became thrown out almost beyond the Sun's reach. Perhaps, even, they are wandering interstellar bodies captured by the Sun over staggering ages of time. We know that some comets are being flung out of the Solar System altogether by the powerful pull of Jupiter taking over from the Sun's gravity as they pass. Is the same thing happening to other stars? Do cometary bodies pass from one star to another?

We are talking here in terms of millions of years, and we can have no proper grasp of such lengths of time. Most astronomers like to keep things simple, and believe that comets were formed with the rest of the Solar System. But nobody knows, and when a rare bright visitor displays its glory in the sky we can only wonder at the cruel length of its night and the brief brilliance of its day.

6 Stars like the Sun

By everyday standards, the scale of the Solar System is huge. But when we turn our attention to the stars, its size dwindles. We have taken another tremendous jump in scale and numbers. Instead of nine planets separated by just millions of kilometres, we are now surveying thousands of millions of stars separated by millions of millions of kilometres!

There is safety in numbers. When we try to learn something about the stars, we are on much safer ground than the astronomer who is looking into the way the Solar System came into being. This is because he has only one object, or collection of objects, on which to test his ideas. If he asks himself, 'What would the Solar System have been like *if* . . .?' he has to answer the question himself. None of our telescopes can show systems of planets around other stars like the Sun to give him some new ideas.

The stellar astronomer is much luckier. There are so many stars in the sky that he knows he can see almost every type of star that there could be. He can see common stars and rare stars and know that they are common or rare because of their numbers. He can see young and old stars and learn something of their history. This is of great importance. We would know very little about the way a star is formed and dies if we had only the Sun to look at. The stars in the night sky are only points of light, dimmed and shrunk by their huge distances, but together they tell us many things that the Sun cannot. Considering that the largest telescopes in the world cannot show the stars as anything but the tiniest points of light, it is astounding what astronomers have managed to find about them.

Astronomy of the Solar System – the planets, at least – had made some headway even in ancient times. The naked-eye astronomers of a couple of thousand years ago had discovered the 'wandering stars', and worked out that they must be moving around the Earth or the Sun, although nobody finally proved that the Sun is the centre of the planetary family until about 1600. But the stars remain the same from century to century, or so it seemed to most people.

Even after the telescope was invented, astronomers practically ignored the stars for a good many years. All those centuries of taking them for granted had had a bad effect. Most of the time was spent looking at the planets, which showed discs and satellites. The stars were certainly very useful as reference points in the sky for measuring the positions of planets, but nobody seemed to have much interest in them as astronomical objects. People vaguely supposed that the stars were like the Sun, only very far away. Not until about two centuries ago did astronomy of the stars and other objects far beyond the Solar System really begin.

It started with the work of William Herschel, a musician from Hanover, who came to England in 1757 and took up astronomy as a hobby. He made his own telescopes, because he could not buy any large enough, and spent all his spare hours studying the night sky. In 1781 he created a sensation by discovering the new outer planet Uranus. In a way this was an accident, but a very happy one. It brought fame to Herschel and a salary from King George III, which meant that he could spend all his time observing instead of fitting telescopic sessions in with his musical duties.

When the sky was dark Herschel and his telescope searched its depths. Millions of stars passed before his view, bright and faint, white and tinted. Many seemed to be on their own, but others were in pairs, and some were in groups, which surely meant that they were connected in some way. He found dense clusters of stars, their numbers running to thousands. He found stars in patches of milky luminous matter, and other luminous patches on their own. These we know as **nebulae**. Thousands of objects were catalogued, but no great sense came of it all. It was too bewildering. Just looking at the stars told nothing about how bright they really were, or how far away – they were just pinpoints of light against the sky.

But Herschel did find out one very important thing. Some of his pairs of stars – we call them **binary stars** – seemed to be slowly moving round each other as the years passed. It seemed to prove that the same law of gravity that binds the Moon to the Earth, and the planets to the Sun, can hold close stars together. This was a tremendous discovery, one of our first pieces of real knowledge. In the 19th century, progress was much faster. In 1838, the first measurements of a star's distance from the Earth were made, and the true scale of the universe, or at least our small part of it, began to be realized. By about 1860, a wonderful new piece of equipment was being used, something that has made modern astronomy possible. This was the **spectroscope**. The telescope can show faint stars, and measure their positions in the sky with great accuracy. But a telescope with a spectroscope attached can tell us things about the star itself – how hot it is, what elements are in it, how fast it is moving through space, how quickly it spins on its axis, and so on. Most astronomers before this time would never even have thought of asking such questions! A few words must be said about this amazing instrument.

In Chapter 2 we learned a little about electromagnetic radiation. The eye sees colours from red, through orange, yellow, and green, to blue. The difference between these colours is that the distance between the tiny pulses of energy, or **wavelength**, is longer for red light than for blue. The spectroscope spreads the light from an object out into all its different colours and wavelengths.

Starlight is a jumble of wavelengths. All that the eye can do is to see that some are reddish or yellow, while others are white. (Even this tells us something. Red stars are cooler than white ones, just like the coals away from the hot centre of a furnace.) The spectroscope, however, can give the astronomer much more detailed information about these colours; it can examine every one of the thousands of wavelengths in the long line of graded colours, or **spectrum**, that it produces from the star's light. So it can tell the temperature of the star very accurately. It can also say something about the elements in the star, because each element sends out its own particular wavelengths of light. Since these wavelengths are affected by the star's movement, we can also learn about its speed though space and the spinning of its surface, just by examining the details of the spectrum.

With the development of photography towards the end of the 19th century, the stellar astronomer's armoury was practically complete. Instead of struggling to see faint images through his spectroscope, he could photograph them and examine them the next day in comfort, at his desk. The telescope, the spectroscope, and the camera have made possible our present knowledge of the stars. Astronomers have examined the light from tens of thousands of stars in great detail, and they seem to have solved one of the biggest problems of all: how do stars form, and what happens to them during their lifetimes?

Let us take a look now at how astronomers have gone about the problem of how stars develop. With very rare exceptions, we cannot see stars changing before our eyes. They develop over millions of years rather than over days or months. So the ways of the astronomer are very different from the method of a scientist in his laboratory. For example, if we wanted to find out how a flower grows the simplest way would be to plant a seed and watch it develop, taking careful note of what happens. In other words, we should perform an experiment, and it wouldn't take very long to have a complete picture of how a flower seed germinates, the leaves spring up, the bud opens, new seeds form, and the flower finally dies – just by watching one plant during a season.

But suppose that we wanted to see how something very slow-growing, like an oak tree, develops. We could, of course, plant an acorn and wait, but we should never see our tree pass right through its life, or even reach maturity, because oak trees live for hundreds of years. So we cannot perform an experiment. What we can do is to go around some wild moorland, where trees are left to their own devices, and look for oak trees in different stages of development. There we shall find young saplings, spindly adolescents, grown-up trees in the prime of life, and finally ancient, gnarled giants on the verge of death, simply by walking around. Our knowledge will have come from observation alone.

In many ways this matches the position of the astronomer. He cannot perform experiments on the objects that he observes in the sky, but he can study them with care and see which look young and which look old, and try to work out how the various pieces fit into the puzzle. Nowhere is this more true than in the study of the lifetimes of stars. Even so, astronomers were troubled for a long time because they did not know what young and old stars ought to look like! It took many, many years of observing and pondering to come to our present ideas, and nobody would pretend that we have all the answers. But because stars are such important objects in the universe, giving out light and heat and making life on planets possible, we must do our best to paint a picture.

Scattered through our galaxy of stars, with its millions upon millions of suns, we find enormous clouds of gas many light-years across. These are the nebulae which so interested Herschel. In some parts of the sky we see them as dark masses, hiding the stars beyond. Other nebulae are bright, made to shine by the light of nearby stars.

Near many of the nebulae we find small dark spots. The nebulae contain the material for future stars, and these spots are really huge collapsing clouds of gas and dust that will one day turn into stars.

The next stage that we can observe is the very young stars themselves. Here and there we find stars that are not yet hot enough to shine brightly, but they give off heat rays. Our eyes cannot see these rays, but special equipment can detect them, just as the wire in Chapter 2 became warm before it started to glow, and could be sensed by the nerves in the skin. Then we find dim red stars, still smothered in the remains of the nebula from which they formed. These are probably in the same stage as the Sun was when the solar nebula began to condense into planets. Possibly these stars, too, are giving birth to planets as we watch them, but we cannot tell – they are much too far away. No telescope on the Earth could see a planet even at the distance of the nearest star.

What sort of time scale are we thinking of? A star like the Sun would probably be formed from a nebula several hundred times the diameter of the Solar System, and it would take a few million years to collapse to a star-size. After this, however, it might reach the shining stage in just a few thousand years as the infalling gas becomes dense enough to give out heat and light as a faint red star. Some more millions of years may be needed for the nuclear processes to work up full power and the star to shine as an adult.

The formation of stars, between the time when they start to glow and that when they become real suns, must be fairly quick by astronomical standards because not many have been found. Of course, these youthful objects are not yet very luminous, and so they may be difficult to find, but even so there are not many known. This idea of measuring time by assessing numbers may seem a little strange at first, so let us take a down-to-earth example. Suppose that, for some reason, a visitor from space was studying people walking around the streets in the British Isles. He has heard that we have invented a strange toy called a yo-yo, and that everyone, at some time in their life, has a yo-yo to play with. He studies as many groups of people as he can find, but he sees only a very small number playing with a yo-yo, and every one is a child. He draws two conclusions: only children play with yo-yos, and even they do not play with them for very long.

He might be tempted to make another conclusion, which is that the children he sees playing with yo-yos play with them the whole time, until they grow up (he hasn't seen any adult with a yo-yo, so they must stop). But he has already been told that *everybody* sometimes plays with a yo-yo. So the ones he sees are the ones who happen to be passing through that phase when he makes his observations.

We know that every star must have a beginning, and we think that stars are being born in great numbers at the present moment, throughout the Galaxy, to make up for the ones that die. Therefore, if we find only a few infant stars, we can assume that they pass through this stage very quickly.

The crowds of stars that shine in the night sky can be sorted out into groups. Mainly we can group them by colour – white, pale yellow, full yellow and reddish. The spectroscope puts all this into much more detail, and finds many other types of groups. But colour is a useful guide because it tells us straight away that some stars are hotter than others. However, this misled astronomers for a long time. They thought that a star grows slowly from its dim red state to a bright red state, then to yellow, and then to white at the peak of its power, finally dimming down to yellow, red and final extinction. In other words, they believed that colour was just connected with age.

We now know that this is wrong. A star grows up and begins its adult life in not more than a few million years. It starts turning hydrogen into helium, and just keeps going without much temperature change until the hydrogen supplies begin to run down. So stars are reddish, yellow or white at the beginning of their adult lives. The colour means a different type of star rather than a different age, and the thing which decides the sort of star it is going to be is the size of the original cloud that condenses.

We can grade stars in terms of mass. The mass of a star is a measure of the amount of material in it. A star whose mass is about that of the Sun will become a Sun-like star, yellowish-white in colour, with a temperature at the surface of about 6,000°C. If it were twice as massive it would shine with a pure white light, and the surface temperature would be about 10,000°C. At four times the mass of the Sun we should find a searing, blue-white object at about 15,000°C. Stars hotter and more massive even than this are known, but they are very rare. At the other end of the scale are found small cool stars, down to perhaps only a tenth of the mass of the Sun. Their surfaces are at about 3,000°C, and they glow redly.

As we might expect, the massive, very hot stars are also

the brightest. Some of them are many thousands of times as luminous as the Sun. We call these stars white or blue giants. The small red stars may be only one hundredth as bright as the Sun, and we call them **red dwarfs**. We do not know much about red dwarfs because they are so faint and difficult to find. For all we know, even smaller and fainter stars may be common, if only our telescopes were powerful enough to find them. This series of stars, from bright white ones to dim red ones, is called the **main sequence**, and the law of the main sequence is 'the whiter, the brighter'.

This, then, is our family of adult, steady stars, burning up their nuclear fuel at full power. Most of the stars that we see in the night sky, either with the naked eye or using a telescope, belong to the main sequence. Something else that we have found out about these stars is that the hottest ones have the shortest lifetimes. Massive stars become so hot and brilliant that they overspend their resources in a startling way, and the lifetimes of some white, very luminous stars may be measured in terms of just a few million years, while the gentle Sun and its fellows simmer away their much smaller stockpiles over thousands of millions of years.

What is the next stage in the lifetime of a star? We have followed it as it first condenses, heats up, and shines brightly at its appointed level. How does old age creep up on it?

Helium, the element that is produced by the star in its nuclear engine, is denser than hydrogen, and so it sinks to the centre of the star. As more hydrogen is converted, this core of helium grows larger. Old age begins for the star when this core reaches a certain size; it then stops growing, and even shrinks slightly. This contraction makes the core heat up to an even higher temperature than it was at before. The increased radiation causes the outer layers of the star to expand, and as it expands the surface cools and becomes redder. This expanded, reddened star we call a **red giant**. Its surface temperature may be as low as that of a red dwarf star, but because it has grown so huge the whole star shines much more brightly than a red dwarf.

It is fortunate indeed that we shall not be here to witness such a transformation of the Sun. It will be thousands of millions of years before its helium core grows so large that it starts to contract. But once this does happen, a terrifying fate will befall the inner planets of the Solar System. Their parent will grow and swallow them – Mercury, Venus, and perhaps even Earth will disappear into the searing gases of the distended star. Meanwhile, the core will grow hotter and hotter as the helium itself begins to transform itself into other elements, such as carbon and oxygen. It was at a temperature of about sixteen million degrees Centigrade when the Sun was shining steadily, but now it may have reached 100 million degrees or more.

The end probably comes quite suddenly. Perhaps there is a sudden blast of radiation from the core that hurls these outer layers of hydrogen off into space. The core cannot now get any hotter, because it has lost its overcoat, and so it cools – and collapses. Its brightness dwindles as it dies. Smaller and smaller it shrinks, until it is no bigger than a planet. The density of matter becomes enormous, much heavier than anything known on the Earth; a sugar-cube sample of the material would weigh hundreds of kilograms. The star has neared the end of its visible life as a **white dwarf**.

White dwarfs are very faint indeed, and we can see only the ones within a few light-years of the Sun. But it seems that most stars must end their lives in this way, as shrunken, cooling globes of matter. The material that collected before their birth as dancing hydrogen atoms, as thin as a comet's tail, has now been through the unimaginable fury that rages at the centre of a star. Atoms have been stripped, reassembled, stripped again, remoulded – and now crushed by their own weight. No power in the universe could restore them. These dying white dwarfs whirl on and on through space, finally becoming dark and dead black dwarfs, invisible ghosts with a future of cheerless eternity.

7 Stars unlike the Sun

In the last chapter we looked at the way in which stars are formed, spend their adult life, pass into old age, and die. Every star in the Galaxy goes through something like this history although, as we shall see, some die more splendidly than others. But not all stars are safe and steady, like the Sun. We call them **variable stars**, because their brightness changes. Others are unlike the Sun because they are in pairs or small groups – we call these **double** or **multiple stars**. Others again are in clusters, which may contain thousands of stars. We must say a few words about all of these.

Double and multiple stars

The moment astronomers began turning telescopes to the sky, they found pairs and groups of stars that looked as if they might be real neighbours in space. But it was not easy to tell, because we cannot find out the distance of anything in the night sky just by looking at it. All the stars appear as points of light. If we see two stars side by side in the sky, it might just have happened this way because they are nearly in the same line, as seen from the Earth. To find out if they really are near each other in space, detective work is needed. Since the time when this was first done by William Herschel, many hundreds of these binary stars have been discovered and followed. The double stars which are not really twins at all, but are line-of-sight effects, are known as **optical** double stars. Optical pairs may be spectacular to the observer, but they are not of much interest to the astronomer.

Binary stars are surprisingly common. Probably a quarter of all the stars in the Galaxy are members of double systems. Sometimes we find very complicated cases, with binary pairs revolving around other binary pairs, producing families of four or even six stars.

Imagine for a moment what our skies would be like if the Sun were a member of a binary system. Its companion might be a yellowish-white twin, the two slowly twisting around each other as they pass across the sky. They might be many millions of kilometres apart, taking several days to go around each other, or they could be almost touching, distorted by frightful gravitational forces into egg-shaped bodies whirling round their dizzy course in just a few hours (double stars follow the same sort of law as do planets: the closer together they are, the faster they must move).

Then again, the Sun's companion might be in a very different state. It could be less massive, a globe tinged with red and perhaps only half the size. Or it might be a massive star that has passed out of steady adulthood into the old age of a red giant. Now the picture would be more sinister. A huge bronze-coloured, hazy mass, threatening to engulf the Sun entirely, would cast its scorching red heat over our planet. Life – supposing it were possible – would be lived in a world of orange tints until the fiery sunset brought back the stars and we could recover in the refreshing cool of the night.

These ideas are probably completely fanciful. The orbit of a planet around a double star would be so complicated that it might never settle down to a steady pattern. Even if it did, the changing cycles of heating and cooling, day and night, might well make the development of any life forms quite impossible. It is tempting to think that planetary systems belong to single stars, and that binary systems form instead only if the original cloud has enough material in it. We are at least sure that binary stars must have been formed together, so that the companions are of the same age. The fact that we often find these stars to be of completely different types was early evidence that stars really do differ amongst themselves.

We can speculate on what life near a binary star would be like, and marvel at the colour contrast (such as yellow and bluish-white) in many telescopic pairs. Amateur astronomers never tire of looking at these objects. But double stars have been useful to astronomers in another way. If two objects in space are revolving around each other, and we measure how far apart they are, the time they take to go around each other once gives us the mass of the two objects. It is not so easy to work out the mass of each separate star, but knowing the mass of the pair can be very useful.

This method can also be used backwards. If we do not know the distance of a binary star, we can make a guess at its mass from the colours of the stars. Using the orbital period, we can then work out their real separation in kilometres. If we know this, and the angle between them in the sky – which is easy to measure – it is a simple matter to calculate how far away the binary must be for the stars to look as wide apart as they do.

The periods, or 'years', of binary stars can be almost anything. Some whirl around each other in just a few hours, with their surfaces almost touching. We cannot separate such close objects with any existing telescope, but they may show up as a variable star, as we shall see on page 107. The period of the closest observable binary star is just under six years. Some very wide pairs of suns are known to be gravitationally connected, but show such slow motion around each other that a complete orbit might take something like a million years. In between these extremes we find all possible varieties in the many hundreds of binary stars that astronomers have catalogued during the past two centuries.

Star clusters

If we take a small telescope, or even a pair of binoculars, and range carefully across the Milky Way on a dark night, we shall find that here and there stars are clustered together into dense groups. The stars in some of these groups are so close-packed that they appear more as a blur than as separate points, while others are spread more thinly. New and fainter clusters keep on appearing as we build new and more powerful instruments and range deeper into the depths of our star-city.

These clusters are real families of stars, born out of the same gigantic clouds of material. In fact, many astronomers believe that all stars were born in groups. If the cluster is close-packed, with the stars several times closer to each other than the Sun is to its neighbour stars, their gravity may hold them together for thousands of millions of years. Wider apart, though, they will slowly drift apart, and in a few hundred million years the stars will have scattered. This may be what happened in the case of the Sun. If it was born in a family its old relatives must still shine in the sky, but we cannot now tell which ones they were because of the slow mixing with other stars.

Some of the clusters in the Milky Way are so bright that they can be seen with the naked eye. Take the famous group of the Pleiades (see page 137). At least seven of the brightest stars can be made out, and binoculars will show many more. The Pleiades are a young cluster, formed probably not more than twenty million years ago (remember that the age of the Sun is at least four and a half thousand million years!). Here we find about 500 stars of all types. If we make a model with the distance of the Pleiades from the Sun (about 400 light-years) equal to 100 metres, the stars in the cluster will be found to be in a group about five metres across. The Sun's neighbour stars would be represented by other minute points (invisible to the unaided eye, on this scale) about one metre apart. This means that there are about ten times as many stars inside the Pleiades as there are in a similar amount of space near the Sun. The night sky in the Pleiades would be a lot more interesting than ours; but the stars are slowly drifting apart. If we could return to the Earth in a few hundred million years' time and look up at the sky, we should probably notice many differences – the vanishing of the Pleiades cluster would be one of them.

We can tell that the Pleiades stars are of recent birth because they are all very white. White stars, as we have seen, are more massive than the Sun, and run through their fiercely-burning lives quickly, so they cannot have been in existence for long. But other Milky Way clusters look quite different. Take another naked-eye group, the Hyades cluster, which is not far away from the Pleiades in the sky (see page 137). We do not find bright white stars in this group, but many reddish ones. It seems that the white and massive stars have already burnt themselves out and passed into the red giant stage, leaving only the 'steady' yellowish-white and cooler stars to burn on. The Hyades must be much older than the Pleiades – perhaps a thousand million years old. Some other clusters look even older than this. They have survived so long as clusters because their stars are packed much more closely than the ones in the Pleiades. In this way, clusters tell us a great deal about the development of different types of stars.

These fairly scattered, gradually decaying groups of stars are known as **open clusters**. They seem to be forming all the time, giving birth to new stars in the Galaxy as old ones die. The other type of cluster known to astronomers, **globular clusters**, are quite different. Open clusters may contain just a few hundred stars; globular clusters contain tens of thousands, massed into a huge ball. These gigantic swarms of stars, of which about a hundred have been discovered, form an outer shell around our Galaxy. Globular clusters contain many old stars, and may have been formed right back at the time of the Galaxy's own origin.

Variable stars

As we have seen, the Sun appears to be a steady, unexciting star. It is just as well for us that it is, for the flarings and dimmings that we see in many night-sky stars would rule out any living forms in their neighbourhood. The Sun seems to have shone with a constant output for hundreds or even thousands of millions of years, but we know of many stars that change noticeably in brightness in periods of years, days or even hours.

Some of these variable stars are in fact a binary pair seen edge-on (*figure 22*). These pairs are so close together that they appear as a single star even through the largest telescopes, and this 'star' will dim down if one member of the binary passes in front of the other and so blocks out part of the light. We call these objects **eclipsing binaries**, and some are spectacular to watch because a large change of brightness can happen in half an hour or so if the stars are close together and fast-moving.

How do we know that there are two stars, if they are seen only as one? The answer lies in the spectroscope. Nothing seems to be denied this light-sifting instrument. By spreading out and analysing the light from an eclipsing binary it can tell us what sort of stars are involved and even how far apart they are!

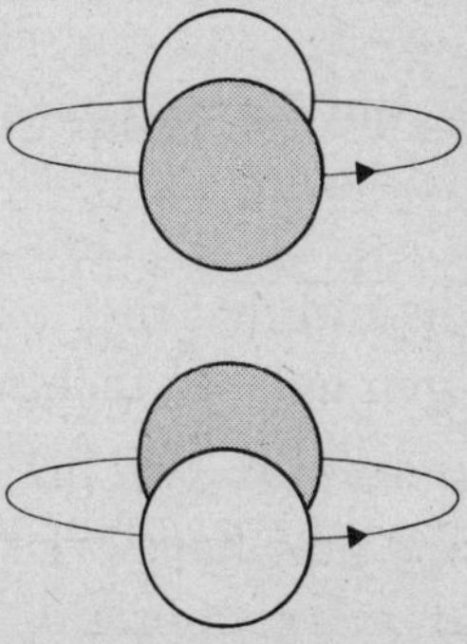

Figure 22 If two stars are revolving around each other almost edge-on, the light reaching the Earth will be cut down when one passes in front of the other. The light-drop will be greatest in the upper position, when the dimmer star of the pair partly blocks out the brighter one

However, eclipsing binaries are not really changing their light output. Other stars really do brighten and fade often because they are pulsating in and out like a balloon that is blown up and let down in a regular way. It may take several months for one 'breath', and these slowly-pulsating stars are known as **long-period variables**, or LPVs. Astronomers believe that many ageing stars pass through this phase on their way to becoming red giants, a their hot centres repeatedly puff up the outer layers. These LPVs all have a reddish colour, and the change in brightness can take place many thousands of times. We find other pulsating stars too, yellower, brighter and faster-changing than the LPVs. These are called Cepheids, and there will be more to say about them in the next chapter.

Some stars change in brightness because they are close binary systems – not eclipsing, but passing clouds of hot gas from one to the other in an explosive way. This means that we see sudden surges of brightness ('sudden' means in a day or two) every few weeks or months. Once again we have no hope of seeing these pairs in action, but this idea is the best explanation for the outbursts. These stars are often called **dwarf novae**, because they do in a small wa what the real **novae** do much more spectacularly.

A nova is a star – probably a member of a binary system, but we are concerned here only with the one star – going through a critical stage in its lifetime. Every year, several stars in the Galaxy which are more massive than the Sun find that they have burnt enough of their hydrogen to leave themselves with a large core of helium. A star is all the time performing a delicate balancing-act between the roaring heat of its core and the much cooler surface gases. If the core suddenly cooled slightly, the surface would collapse inwards; if it heated up too much, the outer part of the star would be blasted away. Astronomers believe that a nova occurs when the core becomes too large and too hot. The balance is upset. Triggered by the attraction of its companion star, colossal pulses rend the surface. In a matter of hours these pulses become so big that the star cannot hold the outer layers down, and they are flung outwards.

An astronomer on the Earth is scanning some photographs of the night sky, comparing two pictures taken some weeks apart. Suddenly his attention is drawn by a star showing on his last photograph which does not appear on the one taken before. He checks atlases and catalogues. Finally he finds the star on an old and detailed chart, as a tiny speck. The astronomer knows that he has found a nova: that tiny speck of a star has blasted its way up in brightness, a jump of ten thousand times or even more. For a few nights it will shine out. Then, as the wrecked layers cool and dim, the star fades back to the brightness it had before. The fading will take years, although the outburst took only a few hours. In 1975 one of the brightest novae for many years shone out as a naked-eye star in the constellation Cygnus.

Stellar suicides

This chapter about strange and unusual stars ends with the most violent type of all – the **supernovae**. A supernova is a star bent on its own destruction. Massive and fiercely hot, it has burnt its hydrogen to helium. Because it is so massive and the pressure within so great, the temperature at the centre rises to hundreds of millions of degrees as the helium collapses on itself. Atoms are ransacked, split and re-formed, again and again. Carbon, oxygen, iron and other elements come into existence. The shrinkage becomes faster and faster, and finally the core collapses completely. The rest of the star – not just the outer layers, as with a nova – is hurled out into space by the tremendous wave of energy. Only the dead, or 'degenerate', core is left.

In the year 1054, Chinese astronomers observed a star that suddenly shone out in the constellation of Taurus, the Bull, as brightly as the planet Venus. Modern astronomers have studied the place in the sky where this object was observed, and they find there a smudge of light now known as the Crab Nebula. The star observed by the Chinese was one of the few supernovae ever recorded in our Galaxy, and the nebula, still visible with a small telescope, is the star's material flying out into space at speeds of many kilometres a second.

At the centre of this cloud is a faint star, the old core of the supernova. We now call it a **neutron star**. A neutron is the heavy particle remaining when an atom is stripped right down, and the core of a supernova is just this – stripped atoms. A neutron star is the densest possible object in the universe, and a piece no bigger than a pin's head would probably weigh as much as an ocean-going liner. The whole core has shrunk to a body only a few kilometres across, flickering as its patchy, white-hot surface spins at the incredible speed of several turns a second. We call this flashing object a **pulsar**.

Here now is something which should bring at least a part of astronomy down to this Earth of ours. We might say: what does it matter how stars are formed, live and die? As long as we have the Sun, the rest of the universe could be wiped out and our lives would not be changed very much. Up to a point, this is true. But if massive stars like the supernova of 1054 had never blasted their material into space, would we be here at all to ask questions?

The reason is this. It was once thought that when the universe began (whenever that was), all the different elements that we know to exist and from which everything, living cells included, is built up, suddenly came into existence. But when physicists began to understand the way in which stars produce their energy they realized that every known element could have been built up in the atom-stripping and reassembly that goes on in the hottest stars. They could all have come from nothing but clouds of hydrogen, the simplest element of all.

A star like the Sun will never be much of an element producer. But it *contains* many elements, and so does the Earth. Where did these elements come from? Perhaps from ancient supernova explosions thousands of millions of years ago? The solar nebula, in which the Sun and planets condensed, must have contained all the elements that we find in the Sun and on the Earth today. It seems quite possible that much of this nebula came from the wreckage of a star: the sort of wreckage that we see as the

Crab Nebula. If this is right, then the cells of our bodies, the food we eat and the air we breathe, the wood, stone and iron that we build with – everything which makes up our world, except for the hydrogen atoms locked away in water molecules – came into being during the digestive processes of a star, forged in the unimaginable heat of tens or hundreds of millions of degrees and blasted out in the fury of countless millions of hydrogen bombs. Who could not be humbled by such a thought?

8 Our Galaxy,
and the 'star-cities' of space

Now that we know something of the life and death of a
star, we are in a good position to look at our star-city, or
Galaxy, and the objects we find in it. But astronomers
have had great trouble in learning how the pieces of our
Galaxy – the stars and the huge clouds or nebulae – fit
together. The difficulty has been because we are inside it
all. We cannot enjoy a general, long-distance view of the
millions of stars that swarm together, and appearances
from the region of the Solar System can be misleading.

The position is rather similar to that of a person looking
out from a high tower over a town, at night. Everywhere
he looks, he sees twinkling lights. Some are bright and
others faint, some are coloured and others are white. He
has no direct idea of which are near and which are far,
except that on average the distant ones will appear
fainter. But an unusually powerful distant light may look
close, while very dim close lights will appear to be far

away. He cannot tell much unless he knows the power or luminosity of each different light that he sees.

Without going out and measuring them, our observer does not know the luminosity of any of the lamps that he sees. But if he is clever, he can partly overcome this drawback. He studies the lights to see if he can find any groups that resemble each other. For instance, he may have some yellow sodium street lamps nearby. They run in lines along the roads. He then looks for other lights of the same colour, running in lines. When he finds them, he assumes that their luminosity is exactly the same as the luminosity of the much closer lamps. By measuring how bright they *appear*, he can work out how much further away they are than the nearby ones. If he can somehow find out what their luminosity really is, he can work out their distance in metres or kilometres.

This simple example tells us something about the astronomer's problems and methods. He has to try to work out the size and form of the Galaxy from the brightness and distribution of the stars in the sky.

The starting-point is to find out as much as possible about the nearby stars, because they can be examined in the greatest detail. Distances must be found first, because if we know how far away a star is, it is not difficult to calculate how luminous it must be. The most direct way of finding the distance of a star is to measure its **parallax** (*figure 23*). To do this, the astronomer carefully photographs the star that he believes to be nearby against its background of much more distant stars (E1). Six months later, when the Earth has moved to the opposite side of its orbit around the Sun (E2), he takes another photograph. The shift of the Earth (about 300 million kilometres)

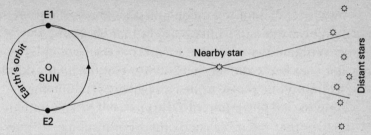

Figure 23 This is a very exaggerated drawing, showing how the Earth's motion around the Sun makes a nearby star appear to move compared with distant stars beyond

makes the star appear to have moved slightly against the very distant background stars. By measuring the amount of this parallax, the distance of the star can be worked out.

These shifts are very small. Even the nearest star to the Sun seems to move against the background by no more than the thickness of a human hair seen about ten metres away! Astronomers can measure parallaxes down to the equivalent of a human hair at about 500 metres, which means that the star is about 200 light-years away. From this nearby sample we have found out a great deal about how luminous stars are, and we can use other stars like them to measure much greater distances that could never be tackled by the parallax method.

Some of the most useful stars of all for this work are the pulsating variable stars mentioned in the last chapter. They are known as Cepheids because one of the first to be identified lies in the constellation Cepheus. Cepheids are very luminous giant yellow stars, and they can be seen a long way away. The remarkable thing about them is that their light changes are in a type of code that astronomers have managed to crack, because the time that a Cepheid takes to go through its cycle of bright to faint and back to bright again (usually a day or two) tells us how luminous it is. Once again, if its brightness as seen from the Earth is measured, its distance can be worked out. Cepheids are easy to pick out amongst the millions of stars that appear on Milky Way photographs, since their brightness changes from one picture to the next, drawing attention to them.

In these ways, fairly large distances can be measured. But the *form* of the Galaxy is another problem. If we are hemmed in at the centre of a crowd of people, we cannot find out much of what is going on towards the edge of the crowd, even though we might have some idea of how big it is. If we could hang over the crowd in a helicopter, we could see everything clearly. Astronomers bemoaned their inconvenient position, but could do little to help themselves until it was realized that we can see other galaxies in the night sky – some of which must surely resemble our own. Using this assumption, observations of our own surroundings began to make better sense.

This understanding came only half a century ago. For a long time before that, observers had been fascinated by the wispy patches of light known as nebulae that were scattered all over the sky. Some were bright (one in the constellation of Andromeda can be seen with the naked eye), but most were faint, and to these faint ones there seemed to be no end. As larger telescopes were built, more and more were detected. Some were clearly clouds of glowing gas connected with stars inside our Galaxy, but most gave no clue to their nature. Most showed no detail. Some of the larger ones seemed to have a spiral form. A few people thought that they might indeed be very distant star-cities, far beyond our own grouping of stars. Others thought that they were stars condensing from clouds of gas, well inside our Galaxy.

Until 1924, there was no way of telling the distance of any of these objects. But in that year, using what was then the largest telescope in the world, the big new two-and-a-half metre aperture telescope at Mount Wilson, in California, the problem was solved. Photographs of the object in Andromeda showed it to be made up of stars scattered along spiral arms, and amongst these stars were variables that behaved exactly like Cepheids. Astronomers had already found out how luminous these Cepheids must be, because the ones in our galaxy had been measured. By using these and other bright stars as indicators, the distance of the Andromeda Galaxy is now estimated at about two-and-a-quarter million light-years, its diameter at about 130,000 light-years.

This is one of the nearest galaxies to our own. Hundreds of others more distant have been examined in detail, and millions have been photographed as tiny smudges of light out to distances of many thousands of millions of light-years. Our Milky Way galaxy, containing perhaps fifty thousand million stars, is just one amongst all these star-cities.

Our own Galaxy is probably slightly smaller than the one in Andromeda. It would take a ray of light about a hundred thousand years to cross it, which means that if we represent the whole Solar System by a pin-head, the diameter of the Galaxy would be about 150 kilometres, the distance from London to Bristol. Some idea of its form is shown in *figure 24*. The central 20,000 light-years or so bulge out into something like a ball. From this centre extend the spiral arms. There are probably only two arms,

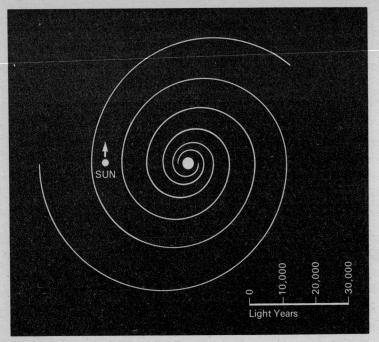

Figure 24 The form of our Galaxy

but they are very long and wind around the centre for
perhaps three complete turns. The Sun seems to lie near
the inner edge of one of these arms, about halfway in from
the edge of the Galaxy. These arms are not more than a
few hundred light-years thick, so that the grouping,
outside its central bulge, is very flattened. When we look
at the Milky Way, we are looking along the nearby arms
of the Galaxy.

The view of our Galaxy is very poor. Within a few
thousand light-years of the Sun, astronomers are fairly
sure that they can see everything. Beyond this, problems
arise. Vast clouds of black or shining gas blot out huge

regions, especially towards the centre of the Galaxy (which is fortunate, because otherwise the masses of stars in the bulge might shine as brightly as the Moon when full!). So most of what we know about galaxies comes from looking at nearby ones. The galaxy in Andromeda shows very well the difference between the stars in the bulge and those in the arms. Towards the centre we find mostly red giants – old stars. In the arms there is a mixture of young white giant stars, steady Sun-like stars and dying white dwarfs (though these are too faint to be made out singly), red giants, and novae, with occasional supernovae (only one has ever been observed, in the year 1885). There is also a great amount of gas and dust in the arms, for the birth of new stars.

Our Galaxy, the Andromeda galaxy, and several other smaller and fainter star-cities, form a cluster of galaxies known as the Local Group. About twenty members are now known, spread over some three million light-years. Only three are big spirals, like our own. Most are **elliptical**, like the central part of a spiral galaxy without the arms, while some are **irregular**, without any real shape at all. Two small irregular galaxies less than two hundred thousand light-years away can be seen with the naked eye by observers in the Earth's southern hemisphere. They look like separate patches of the Milky Way, and are known as the Magellanic Clouds.

Elsewhere in space we find other clusters of galaxies. Some seem to contain hundreds of members, others are just small groups. Every galaxy contains millions of stars, and numbers and distances keep increasing in a bewildering way. If we return to our model, with the Solar System the size of a pinhead and the Galaxy 150 kilometres across, the furthest limits of the universe that we have probed would be about forty times the distance from the Earth to the Moon!

When we survey this inconceivable volume of space, two very interesting things are found. The spectroscope supplies the clue to the first. Light travels as tiny pulses which move through space at 300,000 kilometres a second. The colour of the light depends on the distances between the pulses, which is about four ten-thousandths of a millimetre for the colour blue, and about seven ten-thousandths for red. If something, such as a star or a galaxy, is moving away very fast from the person looking at it, these pulses will be 'stretched' slightly because the light source has moved away a little between each pulse. The wavelength is made slightly longer than it would be if the source remained still, and a longer wavelength means a redder colour. This effect is called a **red shift**. If the object is approaching the observer instead of travelling away from him, the pulses are squashed slightly closer together. The wavelength is shortened, and the colour turns bluer, giving a **blue shift**.

These red and blue shifts can be measured only when the speed involved is several kilometres a second, and even then the precision of a spectroscope is needed to detect it. Our eyes could not notice any change of colour unless the speed reached thousands of kilometres a second. Some objects in the universe are certainly moving as fast as this, but they are too faint to be seen except on photographs taken with giant telescopes.

All the galaxies and clusters of galaxies that we can see in the night sky (apart from the ones in the Local Cluster) show a red shift. The galaxies which appear to be further away, because they appear both smaller and fainter, show larger red shifts, which means that they are moving away faster than the nearby ones. The furthest objects that astronomers can detect are travelling away from us at about three-quarters of the speed of light, and may be as much as 10,000 million light-years away. No galaxies of the ordinary type could possibly be detected at such a huge distance: these objects are the strange, super-luminous bodies known as **quasars**, which seem to emit far more energy than several galaxies put together!

Let us have a look at what this 'expanding universe' idea means. Galaxies are flying apart, as if from an explosion. Can we find out any more about it than that? Certainly we can, if we track back in time. Astronomers have studied very carefully the speeds and distances of hundreds of galaxies, and if we go back about 17,000 million years in time, it looks as if all the galaxies must have been close together. Is that how the universe began, as clouds of hydrogen that suddenly began flying apart? If so, what caused the explosion?

These are questions that astronomers may never be able to answer, but it is possible to make a check on the explosion idea. Objects near the limit of our telescopes are up to 10,000 million light-years away. This means that we are seeing them now as they were 10,000 million years ago, not long after the 'big bang' must have happened. If everything was once close together, and began expanding, then these very distant objects, galaxies and quasars, should look more close-packed in space than galaxies nearer to us. Such observations are very difficult to make, but it certainly does seem as if they are closer together, and that the galaxies in the universe are flying apart as the ages pass.

These visible limits of the universe mark the frontiers of our knowledge, in both space and time. What happens beyond? New instruments being built, some for launching into space, may tell us. Or perhaps it will always be beyond our knowledge. We need not be ashamed if it is. We have not done badly to find out so much, in so short a time, from our dust-speck of a world in the dreadful loneliness of space.

9 Observing with the naked eye

After reading this far you may want to have a look around the sky yourself so as to see the constellations and identify the planets. This chapter is all about how to find the different constellations. Even if you are lucky enough to have a telescope, it cannot be used properly until you know where to point it, so first things first!

Without a knowledge of the brighter stars, and of the general positions of the constellations, the sky will never make sense. It will just be a baffling mass of twinkling points – the clearer the sky, the more confusing it will be. The main patterns of the constellations are not difficult to learn if you have the right help, and a knowledgeable friend is the best of all. If you have one, you are lucky. If you do not know anyone with this knowledge, the information here should help.

On their own, maps of the night sky are not very useful. It is difficult to compare one of these with the real view of the sky. Probably many people have tried and given up, convinced that star-gazing is too difficult for them. The directions in this chapter should give a fairly accurate idea of where some of the brighter stars are to be found. Once you have made out a few 'landmarks' in the sky, the other stars will fall more easily into place than if you are all the time wondering if you made a mistake right at the beginning.

One difficulty in working out the star patterns is that they appear in different parts of the sky at different times of the year, even though we may be observing at the same hour of the night. For example, on an early spring evening, as soon as it gets dark, the Great Bear (often called the Plough) will be overhead. Another look on an autumn evening at the same time will find it low in the north, almost touching the horizon. So we cannot give simple instructions to 'look in such-and-such a direction at such-and-such a time, and you will see this particular star or constellation', because it depends also on the time of the year. In fact, many constellations are completely invisible for three or four months of the year, because the Sun has moved into their region and they are above the horizon only during the day.

Let us try to find out why this is so. *Figure 25* is a view of the Earth's orbit around the Sun, as seen in imagination from somewhere out in space. We are looking from the north side of the orbit, and so the Earth is going around the Sun in an anti-clockwise direction. Of course, the drawing is not to scale. The Earth circles its orbit in a year, and the divisions against the orbit each represent a month. A well-known star group, Orion (the Hunter), is shown. Remember about the scale; the stars in Orion,

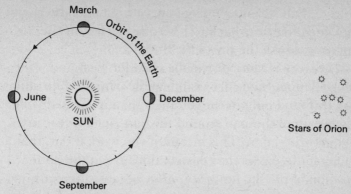

Figure 25 Why Orion can be seen only in wintertime. On this scale, its stars should be placed many thousands of kilometres away!

some of which really do form a cluster in space, should be placed clear of the Earth altogether if we take this size for the Sun.

Half of the Earth is in sunshine, the other half is in night, with a wide twilight zone in between. Stars can be seen only from the night half. When can we see Orion? Starting in December, we find that Orion can be seen very well, because it is on the opposite side of the Earth to the Sun. As the Earth's spin on its axis makes the Sun set in the west, so Orion is rising in the east. Three months later, in March, Orion's direction has drawn nearer to the Earth's twilight zone. It now lies to the left of the Sun in the sky, and sets in the west not long after darkness has fallen. By April it has been lost in the twilight.

Throughout spring and summer, Orion faces the day side of the Earth (round about 15 June, the Sun lies where his head is), but by September the Earth has moved round far enough for Orion, now to the right of the Sun in the sky, to rise in the morning before the sky grows light.

125

Throughout the autumn he rises earlier and earlier, and by Christmas he is back to where he started, at the opposite side of the sky to the Sun.

The story is more or less the same for every constellation. Some are visible in the winter while others will be found only in the summer. All appear to do one big circuit of the sky, around the Sun, once a year in a westerly direction. This means, if you work it out, that as each month passes the constellations are in the same position in the sky *two hours earlier*, because there are twelve months in the year, and twenty-four hours in the day. On a day-to-day basis, the stars return to their positions *four minutes earlier*, and this can be allowed for if you are observing at times different from the standard ones given here.

The constellations are seen best when they are due south in the sky. This is because they are highest above the horizon when south. (A few star groups are always in the northern sky and never set at all, but we shall mention them in a moment.) So we can start identifying the brightest stars by making up a table showing the times of the year when they are due south (it is on pages 186–7). Once we know the direction in which to look, the other piece of information needed is their height, or **altitude**, at this time. Altitude is reckoned in degrees (°). An altitude of 0° means that it is as low as a sea horizon, or the horizon in very flat country. An altitude of 90° is directly overhead, known technically as the **zenith**. Halfway from horizon to zenith is 45°.

It is not very easy to guess the altitude of something in the sky. Ask a person to point to the zenith, and he will probably be looking at an altitude no higher than 70°.

The safest way is to make a simple gauge. Take a piece of paper or card and make two thick upright marks on it exactly thirty-five centimetres apart. Set it up, and ask someone to hold a measuring tape so that your eyes are exactly one metre away from the paper. These two marks now indicate an angle of exactly 20°. Without moving your head, shut one eye and hold a stick at arm's length in front of the marks. Ask your friend to mark with a pencil where it has to be cut off so that the remaining part just fits in between the marks. When this is done, you have a handy 20° gauge whenever you hold it up at arm's length. Paint it white, or bind white masking tape round it, so that it shows up in the dark. Remember that it is correct only for *your* length of arm; longer arms need longer sticks, and the other way round! You will be able to measure altitudes accurately enough right up to the zenith, if you wish, by working in these 20° sections.

You may already happen to know, quite accurately, where the southern direction is from your observing site. But it is always best to check, using the Pole Star. This can be found by using an ordinary pocket compass, but remember that a magnetic compass points about 8° to the west (left) of true north. This difference is because the mass of iron deep in the Earth that attracts the compass needle is not exactly at the Pole. In fact, it is many hundreds of kilometres away and is slowly moving about, so that as the years pass the magnetic difference changes. But 8° will do for the next few years. Having found this line, use your 20° altitude gauge to find an altitude of just over 50°, which will be about two-and-a-half sections. This should bring your gaze up to the Pole Star, which is the brightest star in that part of the sky.

The Pole Star is the most useful star in the sky because it is always in the same place. All the other stars move slowly around the sky as the seasons change, but the Pole Star remains at the north point of the heavens. Surrounding it are the constellations of the northern sky, including the Great Bear, that never set below the horizon.

Figure 26 explains why this is so. The Earth spins once a day on its axis, and the direction of this axis remains almost the same from century to century. This means that if we could sight along it we should always find it pointing to the same position among the stars. Purely by chance, the north direction of the axis points towards the bright

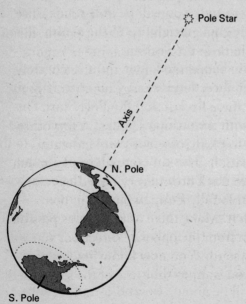

Figure 26 The axis around which the Earth spins happens to point towards a bright star – the Pole Star

star that we call the Pole Star. The south direction of the axis is towards an empty patch of sky, so observers in the southern hemisphere have no pole star worthy of the name.

During the time it takes the Earth to spin on its axis, the constellations seem to move once right round the sky, and they *appear* to move around the Pole Star. Stars and groups that are far from the Pole rise and set in the normal way, but what about the stars that are closer to the Pole Star than the altitude of the Pole above the northern horizon? They can always be seen when the sky is dark. We call these objects **circumpolar**.

Figure 27 shows the brighter circumpolar constellations as they appear at different times of the year, when the observer looks north. The 'saucepan' shape of the Great Bear is familiar to most people, and on the opposite side of the pole is the 'W' shape of Cassiopeia, another famous group. Once you have found these two and the Pole Star, the northern sky will never seem strange again and you will enjoy watching these friends as they slowly turn around each other with the passing seasons. A few other stars are shown too, to fill in some gaps and indicate where other constellations are, but you will need a much more detailed map to track down every naked-eye star!

With the Pole Star found, set up two posts in the ground to line up on it. Make them as upright as possible. Lining up with them from the opposite direction, you will be facing accurately south. You now know in which direction to look if you want to time any of the stars listed in the table.

The star maps with this chapter show the night sky as you will see it when you look up at six different times of

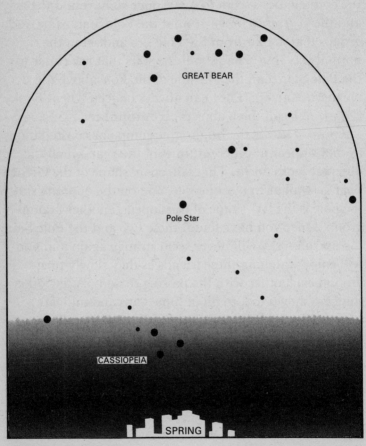

GREAT BEAR

Pole Star

CASSIOPEIA

SPRING

Figure 27 The northern sky in the evening of different seasons in the year, showing how the Great Bear and Cassiopeia gradually swing around the Pole Star

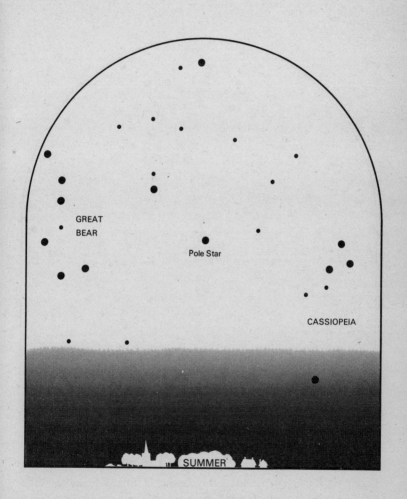

GREAT
BEAR

Pole Star

CASSIOPEIA

SUMMER

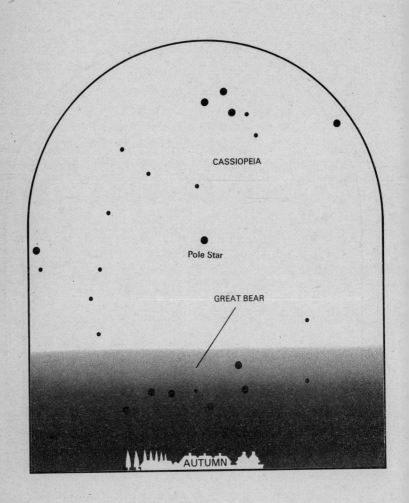

CASSIOPEIA

Pole Star

GREAT BEAR

AUTUMN

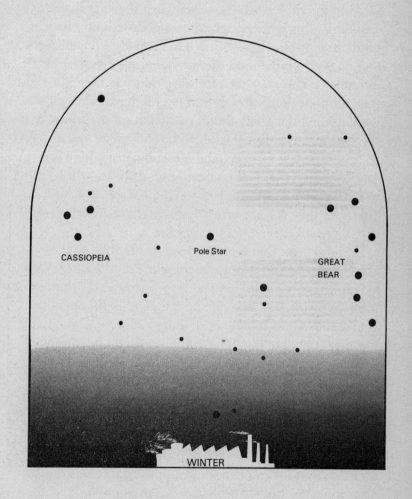

CASSIOPEIA

Pole Star

GREAT
BEAR

WINTER

the year. The circle is the horizon, and the zenith or overhead point is in the middle of each map. Compass directions are indicated. Some of the stars have a name. Most of these are the important sighting stars, which are listed in the table with the times when they are due south. They are all bright enough to be found without much difficulty, even if the sighting is in error by a few degrees, and once they are found the surrounding stars should fall into place. You may even feel sure that you have the right stars without doing any sighting at all, particularly if it is winter when the easily-found constellation of Orion lies in the southern sky. But the table and the gauge are a useful reserve, and it is always handy to know just where the southern direction is. The times and altitudes will be right to within about 5° for any observing site in the British Isles, but they cannot be used abroad because our view of the sky changes if we travel very far.

Suppose now that we want to start identifying the constellations, and it is the evening of 1 September. We look at the table on pages 186–7 for a guide star that is due south at a suitable time. There is a very useful one: the bright star Altair in the constellation of Aquila, the Eagle. On this very date it will be south at exactly twenty-one hours Greenwich Mean Time (GMT), which is 9 pm (10 pm if Summer Time is being used). The altitude is 43°, which is equal to two steps of the gauge and a little bit for luck. If you cannot see a proper horizon from your observing site, find a level piece of ground and set up a post that is the same height as your eyes. Paint the top white so that it can be made out in the dark, and measure your altitudes from this position, as in *figure 28*.
Once you have identified Altair, you can use Map 5 to

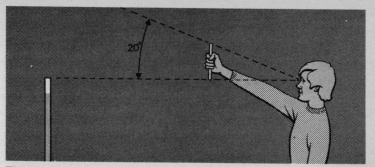

Figure 28 Measuring altitude with a 20° stick

search for other stars and groups. Look for the brightest
ones (the largest dots on the map) first. High in the sky,
slightly towards the west, is Vega, the brightest star in the
constellation of Lyra (the Lyre). Even higher, at the
zenith, is Deneb, the leader of Cygnus (the Swan). Altair,
Vega and Deneb are so conspicuous that they are often
called the Summer Triangle.

   With these three stars as a guide, fainter objects can be
sought. A line from Deneb through Altair brings you near
the south-western horizon, where a group of stars marks
Sagittarius (the Archer). An equal-sided triangle with
Vega and Altair forming two corners finds the brightest
star in Ophiuchus (the Serpent-bearer) at its south-
western corner; and so on. Once you have a few key
markers, you can progress a long way by drawing lines,
triangles and squares in the sky. These are the methods
that will be used long after the naked-eye stars have
become familiar and you are seeking the much fainter
objects that can be found only on detailed atlases.

   Having taken all this trouble to find them, we shall now
say a few words about the stars and constellations that are
shown in each of the pairs of maps that cover the year's

progress of the sky. Incidentally, a pair of binoculars will add greatly to the fun of finding your way around the stars, and it is well worth obtaining or borrowing a pair.

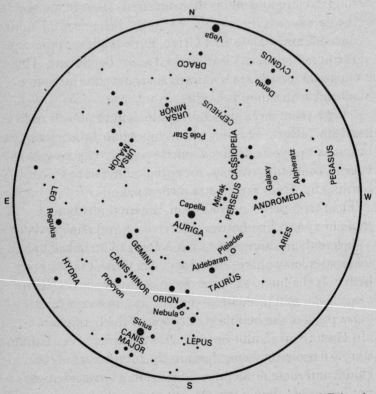

Map 1 30 Dec 23h; 15 Jan 22h; 30 Jan 21h; 15 Feb 20h; 28 Feb 19h

Aldebaran, the leader of Taurus (the Bull) stands due south. This is a red giant star, about sixty light-years away and thirty-five times as large as the Sun. You can easily see its colour with the naked eye. Just to the west of it is the scattered Hyades cluster, and the famous Pleiades cluster is nearby. To the east of the zenith you find Capella, the leader of Auriga (the Charioteer). Capella is another giant star, but much more yellow than Aldebaran. It is about eighty times as bright as the Sun. The Milky Way passes through Auriga, but it is not very bright here compared with the parts that are seen during the summer, because we are looking away from the dense central part of the galaxy.

The fine constellation of Orion approaches south. Look at the upper left-hand star, the red giant Betelgeuse. This is one of the hugest stars known, as massive as thirty-five Suns and larger than the orbit of the planet Mars! It is 240 light-years away. By contrast, look at the lower right-hand star, Rigel. This is a white 'supergiant' star, about as bright as 14,000 Suns and some 600 light-years away. Rigel is probably twice as hot as the Sun, and must be burning up its hydrogen at a furious pace.

The three 'belt' stars of Orion, the mythical hunter, shine in a short line between Betelgeuse and Rigel. About 5° below them shines the Great Nebula. The naked eye sees it as a hazy patch, but binoculars show it much better. It is a huge, glowing cloud of gas about 600 light-years away and three light-years across, but very faint outer parts of the nebula cover most of the constellation, although these cannot be seen with the naked eye. Young stars are probably being born in the bright part of the cloud, and some of the blue-white stars in this group do not look more than a few million years old.

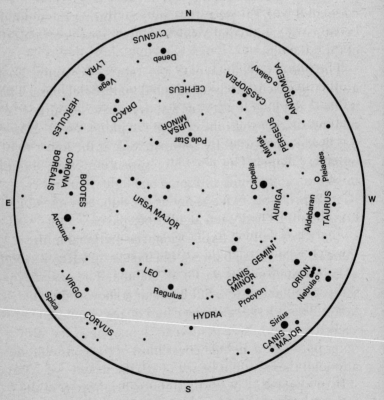

Map 2 28 Feb 23h; 15 March 22h; 31 March 21h

Several bright stars have just passed due south. Take special note of Sirius, the leader of Canis Major (the Greater Dog). You can find it by drawing a straight line eastwards from the two bottom stars in Orion. Sirius is one of the closest stars to us, only eight-and-a-half light-years away and twenty-three times as bright as the Sun. It is a hot white star. Large telescopes show that it has a companion star, the binary pair revolving around each other in fifty years. This companion was the first white dwarf star ever to be observed. Its diameter is probably about the same as that of the planet Uranus, but its mass is nearly as great as the Sun's! The density of this nearly dead, collapsed star is about 5,000 times the density of lead.

Slightly west of south, about 40° up, we find the pale yellow star Procyon in Canis Minor (the Smaller Dog). There is not much to this constellation besides Procyon, which forms a triangle with Betelgeuse and Sirius. About 25° above Procyon are the two stars Castor and Pollux in the constellation of Gemini (the Twins). Castor consists of six stars – three binary systems all revolving around each other.

The summer stars Deneb in Cygnus (the Swan) and Vega in Lyra (the Lyre) are underneath the Pole Star. If you have a clear northern horizon, you should be able to see both of them twinkling low down.

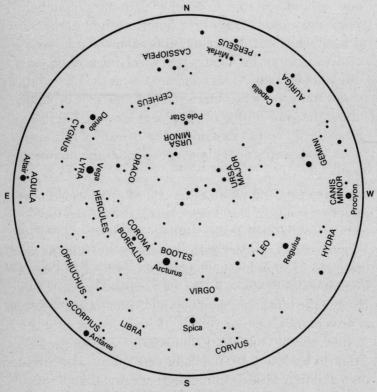

Map 3 15 April 24h; 1 May 23h; 15 May 22h

The short summer nights restrict observing time because you cannot start until fairly late. The Great Bear is now right overhead. At this time of year the southern sky is rather bare, but the leader of the constellation Virgo (the Virgin), the white star Spica, will be easy to find because there are no other bright stars nearby. A long line drawn from Spica to Procyon, in the west, crosses Leo (the Lion). High in the south, and found easily by following the curve of stars in the Great Bear, is the deep yellow giant star Arcturus in the constellation of Boötes (the Herdsman). Arcturus is about forty-five light-years away, and brighter than a hundred Suns. In the northern sky, the 'W' of Cassiopeia is underneath the Pole Star.

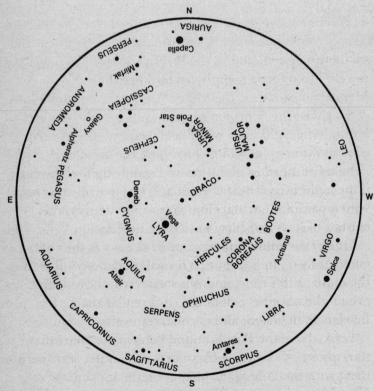

Map 4   15 June 24h; 30 June 23h; 15 July 22h

At this time of year, the region towards the centre of the Galaxy comes into view. Unfortunately it is very near the southern horizon, and in the British Isles we can never see it well. From further south, for instance the Mediterranean area, the Milky Way in the constellations of Scorpius (the Scorpion) and Sagittarius (the Archer) is a wonderful sight even with the naked eye, the massed stars showing up as white clouds and the great dark nebulae outlined as black masses against them. However, if the night is really clear and dark, sweep over this region with a pair of binoculars and you will notice several clusters of stars and hazy patches of nebulae.

One of the most striking stars in the sky is the red giant Antares, in Scorpius. You will find it very low in the south at this time, and binoculars will show its tint even if the naked eye does not. It is redder than Betelgeuse in Orion, and even larger in size.

Look above the Pole Star and you will see two fainter stars about 15° away. A curve of much fainter stars joins them with the Pole Star, making up the small group of Ursa Minor (the Little Bear).

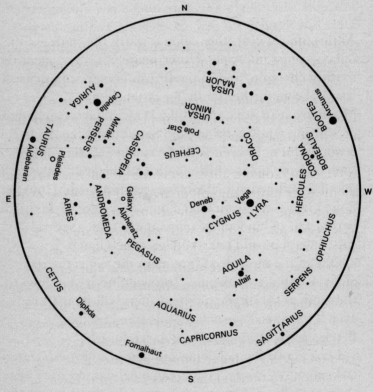

Map 5 15 Aug 24h; 31 Aug 23h; 15 Sept 22h; 30 Sept 21h;
15 Oct 20h

The Summer Triangle is due south in late summer and early autumn, and these three bright stars were mentioned on page 135. See how the Milky Way runs through Cygnus (the Swan) and Aquila (the Eagle) with bright patchiness where the stars crowd. A huge dark nebula runs along this part of the Galaxy, dividing it into two strips. The Milky Way passes on into Cassiopeia, in the east, after which it fades towards Perseus. If you happen to be outside late on the night of 11 August, keep a lookout for Perseid meteors. You will be certain to see several during a half-hour watch, unless the sky is bright with moonlight.

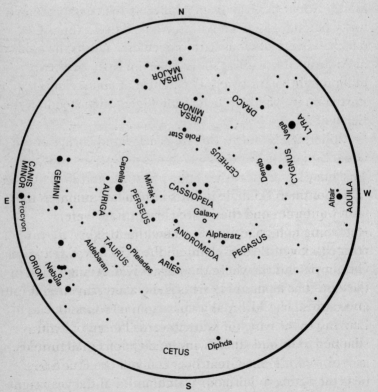

Map 6 31 Oct 23h; 15 Nov 22h; 30 Nov 21h; 15 Dec 20h; 30 Dec 19h

Cassiopeia is now overhead and just below it, to the south, is a line of three stars marking the constellation of Andromeda. Many people find these three stars difficult to make out, but you can time the right-hand star (Alpheratz) from the table, and the other two can then be found. About halfway from Alpheratz to Cassiopeia lies a misty patch, easily seen with the naked eye if the sky is dark, and very obvious with binoculars. This is the galaxy in Andromeda, a spiral system like our own, over two million light-years away. The light that you see now started on its way long before intelligent men stood on the Earth at all.

Alpheratz also forms the upper left-hand corner of the Great Square of Pegasus, which has just passed south. This huge square is rather empty of stars, and so is the rest of the southern sky. Low in the south lies Diphda, in the faint but large constellation of Cetus (the Whale). Returning to high altitudes we find the bright constellation of Perseus, lying in the Milky Way between Cassiopeia and the yellow Capella which is rising high in the east. The leader of Perseus is the white star Mirfak, and binoculars show many stars grouped round it. Looking to the east, the winter constellations of Taurus (the Bull), Gemini (the Twins) and Orion (the Hunter) are rising, while the Great Bear is under the Pole Star, near the northern horizon. With the end of the year comes the end of our cycle of the stars.

10 Amateur astronomy with a telescope

After spending a few evenings looking at the night sky with the naked eye, or using a pair of binoculars, you will be feeling the need for more powerful equipment to reveal the double stars, clusters and nebulae that you have been reading about, as well as showing details on the Moon and planets. You will also find that the star maps in this book do not show enough stars once you have identified the main patterns. The point is, though, that more detailed maps would have been too confusing to start with.

The best atlas to get can be ordered from any bookshop. It is called *Norton's Star Atlas and Reference Handbook* (see Appendix 1). If you are going to take up astronomy in any serious way at all, this book is essential and should be your first purchase.

Unfortunately, the telescope problem is not so simple. There just isn't a convenient, cheap telescope on the market, although there is a lot of very dubious equipment made up to look impressive by manufacturers who have probably never looked at a star in their lives.

Thousands of these instruments, costing perhaps £30, must have been bought by unfortunate people who hoped to see the rings of Saturn and other wonders promised in the advertisements, and found nothing but a shaking blur when the telescope was set up. To be of any use at all, an astronomical telescope must give a sharp image, and it must be steady; most cheap telescopes fail on both counts. A reasonably good new telescope of sufficient power to be useful will cost the best part of a hundred pounds.

Telescope prices have gone up so much in the last ten years that you will always get a better bargain second-hand than new. You could, of course, try to make one, but this would be a big undertaking if you wanted something really powerful. The best answer is a second-hand instrument. There are a surprising number of unused but good telescopes littering houses, attics and garages in this country – so LOOK and ASK. Look in grubby second-hand shops, on advertisement boards, and in the columns of the local paper. Ask your friends and acquaintances if they know of an old telescope anywhere that you could either borrow or buy cheaply. If all else fails, put a 'wanted' advertisement in the local paper. Something is bound to turn up if you persist.

But before starting to search, you should know something about how a telescope works, and what to look out for.

When we look at the sky – or anything else, for that matter – we are using the light that enters the black opening or **pupil** in the middle of each eye. During

149

daylight conditions, the pupil automatically contracts to about two millimetres across to stop the eye from being dazzled. At night it opens up to about eight millimetres across, so as to collect as much light as possible. An astronomical telescope shows fainter stars than we can see without it because the diameter, or **aperture**, of the part collecting light from the sky is larger than the aperture of the human eye. Generally speaking, the bigger the aperture the more powerful the telescope will be. Most telescopes owned by amateur astronomers have an aperture of between 60 and 150 millimetres.

Having collected the light, the telescope focuses it to form an image of whatever it is pointed at. A lens or **object glass**, or a **mirror**, can be used. A lens telescope is called a **refracting** telescope, or just a **refractor**, while a mirror telescope is called a **reflecting** telescope or **reflector**.

The ordinary spy-glass is of the refracting type. The object glass focuses the light to form an image of the object near the other end of the tube (*figure 29*). This image is magnified by a small lens known as the **eyepiece**. An eyepiece works the same way as a strong magnifying glass, and it makes the image produced by the

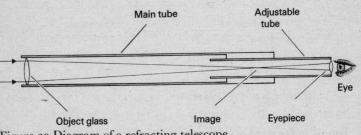

Figure 29 Diagram of a refracting telescope

object glass look bigger, just as it would enlarge any small object held in front of it.

The reflecting type of telescope looks very different, and is used only by astronomers (*figure 30*). The front end of the tube is left open, and a concave (hollowed-out) mirror is placed at the other end, facing the front of the tube. It reflects the light back to form an image, using a small flat mirror placed in the middle of the tube to reflect the light through a small hole cut in the side. The eyepiece is placed here, the observer being side-on to the object he is looking at. There are other types of reflecting telescope, but this is the most common, and it is called a **Newtonian telescope**.

Both these telescopes give upside-down views of the sky. Telescopes to be used for ordinary purposes have extra lenses, or prisms, to give an upright image, but astronomers usually prefer to leave these out because every piece of glass in the light beam dims the image slightly – and light is important where faint stars are concerned.

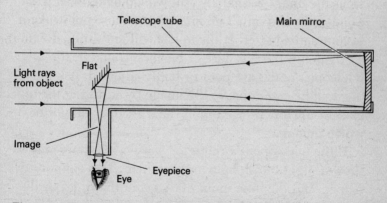

Figure 30 Diagram of a Newtonian reflecting telescope

The length of a telescope does not affect its power. Refracting telescopes are usually longer than reflectors, but this is because of the way they work. A sixty-millimetre aperture refractor might be as long as a 100-millimetre aperture reflector, for instance, with a tube from 80 to 100 centimetres long. The aperture is what matters, together with the quality of the optics and the rigidity of the stand or mounting.

You can see for yourself if the mounting is rigid or wobbly, although even a firm-looking stand may show shake if the telescope is magnifying a hundred times or so. At any rate, some sort of judgment can be made. But nobody can tell the quality of the object glass or mirror without actually using the telescope. If you are thinking of making a purchase, insist on looking through it at a star. Better still, have someone who knows about telescopes look through it. He will see faults that you will not, and he can say if the price is reasonable. If you have no one to guide you, the following points will help.

Point the telescope at a bright star (not a planet), and focus the image as sharply as it will go by moving the eyepiece in and out. The smaller and more point-like it becomes, the better. If the image will not shrink down to a tiny point, but has flare or haziness round it, the telescope's optics are poor or badly adjusted. Ask the owner if he can improve the image by adjusting the object glass or mirror. If he cannot, the telescope will not be worth buying.

If the telescope is a refractor, very bright stars may show a slight bluish halo around them. This cannot be helped, but the blue should be so faint that it is hardly noticeable. If the blue can be seen even around faint naked-eye stars, the object glass is a poor one. Any trace of red in the image, rather than blue, means that the lens is useless for serious work.

These tests should be made with the highest possible magnification. Most telescopes are supplied with two or three eyepieces, each one giving a different power. To find the magnification given by an eyepiece, you divide the **focal length** of the lens or mirror (which is about equal to the length of the tube, but should be marked somewhere, or at least known by the owner) by the focal length of the eyepiece, which once again should be marked on it. For instance, if the mirror or object glass has a focal length of 1000 millimetres, and the focal length of the eyepiece is twenty millimetres, the magnification is 1000/20, or fifty times. A magnification of about 150 for a sixty-millimetre refractor, or 200 for a 100-millimetre reflector, is a good testing power. A useful rule of thumb is to use about twice the number of millimetres in the aperture.

Don't forget that eyepieces can be of poor quality too. If the view is bad, try changing the eyepiece. The advantage of having an astronomical friend to test the telescope is that he can bring along a good eyepiece.

Of course, if you are offered a telescope for nothing, you won't be too critical of its quality. There will probably be something that can be salvaged. But even so, find out as soon as you can if it is a good or a bad one. Many young astronomers have been disappointed with what they see in the sky, only to find out later that their telescope, rather than the sky, was to blame. Because of this, and the general difficulty of knowing how to judge a telescope when you may never have used one before, you cannot be too strongly advised to find someone with the knowledge to help. Remember that the person selling it may really think that it is a good one, just because he doesn't know any better than you do!

To sum up: find out all you can about telescopes by reading about them and, if possible, looking through them. Don't even consider buying a new telescope to start off with. When you have located a second-hand instrument (the likely apertures are 60–75 millimetres for a refractor, and 100–150 millimetres for a reflector), ask an experienced observer to test it for you before you part with the money.

Something else that you should try to do, if you are interested enough to want to buy a telescope, is to join the local astronomical society. Most towns have one. By asking around you may hear of a member with an instrument that he no longer needs, and certainly you will receive all the advice you want. Do not hold back from joining because you don't feel very expert. All societies are more than pleased to have new enthusiasts join; it is what you are keen to do, rather than what you know, that counts. To find out if there is a society in your area, the best course is to contact the central library, which should keep a record of all local societies. If it cannot help, get in touch with the national Federation of Astronomical Societies (Appendix 1).

What sort of observing can you do, once you have obtained a small or moderate-sized telescope? Let us go through the list of interesting objects.

The Sun

Never look through a telescope that is pointing anywhere
near the Sun. You should know enough by now about the
stars to respect their awesome radiation. There is no need
to put your eye anywhere near the eyepiece to observe
sunspots, because an image of the Sun can be projected on
to a piece of white card. Using a magnification of about
fifty times, and holding the screen about thirty
centimetres behind the eyepiece, move the telescope
about until the round disc of the Sun shines on the card.
Focus sharply, and you will be able to see any spots that
are visible. If the focal length of your telescope is 1000
millimetres, the diameter of the Sun's image with this set-
up will be about 130 millimetres, which means that a
sunspot the size of the Earth will be just over a millimetre
across.

You will need to shade the screen from the direct light
of the Sun, otherwise the details in the image will be
washed out. Using a few struts of thin wood, a frame can
be made to hold the screen and leave both hands free for
copying the positions of the spots into the observing book.
A series of daily observations will very soon show the way
that spots form and decay and are carried across the disc
by our star's rotation. The Sun is one of the few
astronomical bodies that can produce something new
almost every day. Do not forget that the image on the
screen has the right and left sides reversed compared with
the way the Sun is in the sky. This means that sunspots
will travel around the disc from right (east) to left (west)
as the Sun rotates.

Eclipses of the Sun, which happen when the Moon
passes in front of it, are very interesting to watch on the

screen. There will be no **total eclipse** visible from the British Isles until the year 1999, but forthcoming **partial eclipses** are given in the astronomical calendar in Appendix 2.

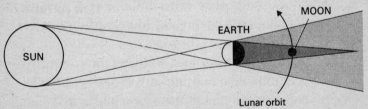

Figure 31 An eclipse of the Moon happens when it passes through the Earth's shadow. The dark central shadow (the umbra) produces the main dimming; the outer part of the shadow (the penumbra) only cuts down the brightness of the Moon slightly

The Moon

This is a wonderful hunting-ground for anyone with the
smallest optical aid, while a good 60–100 millimetre
telescope will show detail down to about five kilometres
across. A magnification of fifty to eighty times will allow
the whole Moon to be seen in the field of view at the same
time, but higher powers will show only a part of the
surface. You will soon become aware of the Earth's
rotation on its axis, which affects every body in the sky;
the Sun and the Moon are both about $\frac{1}{2}°$ across, and they
drift across their own diameter in a couple of minutes.
Even with a low magnification, you will need to adjust the
direction of the telescope every half-minute or so to keep
what you are looking at near the centre of the field of
view, and with high powers guiding has to be almost
continuous. Expensive telescopes are made with electric
motor drives to hold objects in the field of view, a luxury
you are unlikely to be able to afford straight away. What
you will appreciate, though, are slow-motion controls on
the telescope, so that the tube can be moved steadily
along without jerks and vibration.

The Moon map (*figure 31*) will help you to identify some
of the larger craters, mountain ranges and seas.
Occasionally, at full phase, the Moon passes into the
Earth's shadow and turns a dull red-brown colour (*figure
32*). The dates of the next of these **lunar eclipses** are given
in the astronomical calendar (Appendix 2).

Figure 32 This map shows the
Moon in the 'inverted' view familiar
to all astronomers, since astronomical
telescopes reverse the image

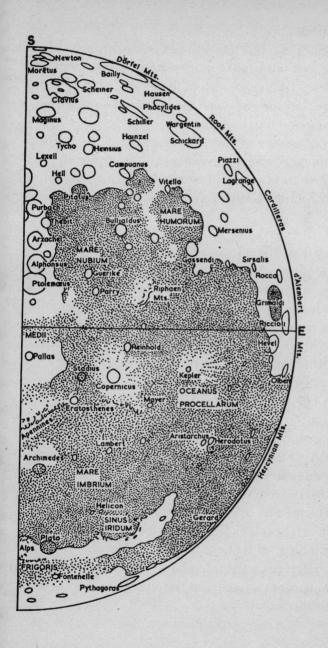

S

Newton
Moretus
Bailly
Dörfel Mts.
Scheiner
Hausen
Clavius
Phocylides
Maginus
Schiller
Wargentin
Hainzel
Schickard
Tycho
Heinsius
Lexell
Hell
Campuanus
Piazzi
Purbach
Pitatus
Vitello
Lagrange
Thebit
Bul[i]aldus
MARE
HUMORUM
Arzachel
Mersenius
Alphonsus
MARE
NUBIUM
Gassendi
Sirsalis
Guerike
Rocca
Ptolemaeus
Parry
Riphaen
Mts.
Grimaldi
Riccioli

Rook Mts.
Cordilleras
d'Alembert Mts.

MEDII
Hevel
Pallas
Reinhold
Stadius
Olbers
Copernicus
Kepler
Mayer
OCEANUS
Eratosthenes
PROCELLARUM
Apennines
Aristarchus
Herodotus
Lambert
Archimedes
MARE
IMBRIUM
Helicon
Gerard
SINUS
IRIDUM
Plato
Alps
FRIGORIS
Fontenelle
Pythagoras

Hercynian Mts.

E

The Planets

Every planet except Pluto will be visible through your telescope, but some make more suitable objects for study than others. To give an idea of their sizes, *figure 33* shows how large they appear when seen through a telescope magnifying one hundred times.

Planet observers will find the *Handbook* of the British Astronomical Association very useful (see Appendix 1). It gives information on the planets' changing position in the sky, their rotation on their axes, and the positions of their satellites.

Mercury is so difficult to see that just sighting it is enough to give satisfaction, and binoculars will be best for finding it in the twilight sky. At eastern elongation, when it is seen in the west after sunset, the best conditions occur in spring because Mercury is then at its highest above the horizon. The best western (morning) elongations, with the planet rising in the east before sunrise, occur in the autumn.

Mercury never sets more than two hours after sunset nor rises more than two hours before sunrise. If you are observing an evening elongation (which will be the case unless you set the alarm clock!), the best time to look for it is about an hour after sunset. Before this, the sky is too bright; afterwards, the planet is too low and is dimmed by horizon haze. The colour of Mercury is white but it often looks pinkish because of the colour of the sky at this time. Start searching for it about ten days before the time of elongation given in the calendar in Appendix 2. There are other elongations as well, but the ones listed are the most favourable.

MERCURY   ☽

VENUS   )

MARS   ○

JUPITER   ◯

SATURN   ♄

URANUS   ∘

NEPTUNE   ∘

Figure 33 If this drawing is viewed
from a distance of 50 cm, it shows
the size the different planets
appear when viewed through a
telescope manifying one hundred
times. Pluto is no more than a
point of light

If you can view the planet with a magnification of fifty to one hundred times you will be able to make out a tiny disc and the phase. At an evening elongation the planet is passing from full to crescent phase. At a morning elongation it starts as a crescent and moves towards full.

Venus is a completely different proposition. It is brighter than any other planet or star, and you will have no difficulty in finding it when it is above the horizon. The crescent phase can be made out using binoculars, and a magnification of seventy-five to one hundred will show a large disc, although the cloudy atmosphere usually means that this disc is just a gleaming white colour.

When brightest, at the thick crescent phase, Venus should be fairly easy to pick up using binoculars in broad daylight, if the sky is a deep blue. It is useless sweeping for it if there is any haze about. Search slowly and with care, making sure that the Sun does not come near the field of view. Once you have picked up Venus, try to see it with the naked eye. This is a good test of sight!

Mars has to be waited for patiently because oppositions are over two years apart. The calendar in Appendix 2 gives details of where it can be found. Mars is interesting to follow because it moves fast in front of the stars, and with binoculars its position can usually be seen to change from night to night.

Mars will appear very small at the next few oppositions (the next really good one, for British observers, will not be until 1988), and a magnification of about 130 will be needed before it looks as large as the Moon seen with the naked eye. If you glimpse a dark marking, try to follow it for an hour or two. It will be moving with the planet's rotation, from east to west (right to left in an inverting astronomical telescope). You should also see whitish clouds or spots near the planet's poles. Do not expect too much, though, because Mars is a very difficult telescopic object.

Jupiter is a real friend. Its disc is so large that it can just be made out with binoculars, and its four large moons will be easily seen as well. An astronomical telescope of the smallest kind will show some of the cloud belts that cross its surface. With a magnification of fifty or more you should be able to see some of the details in the belts. Look out particularly for the Great Red Spot. Sometimes it is so red that the colour can be seen with a small instrument, but in other years it is more like a darkish oval in the southern (upper) part of the disc. Do not be disappointed if you do not see all these details at once. As long as the telescope is a good one, they will appear – but your eye may take time to learn how to see them. You have to train to be an observer just as you must practise to be a runner or a swimmer, and continued practice will make a tremendous difference to what you can see.

Watch the four satellites as they move around the planet from night to night. Sometimes they pass right in front of Jupiter's disc. You may not be able to see them against the bright background, but the shadows that they cast on the surface of Jupiter can often be made out as dark spots. At other times they can pass into Jupiter's shadow, as our Moon passes into the Earth's shadow during an eclipse. When this happens, they will be seen to fade from sight in just a minute or two.

Saturn. You will be able to see the rings with a magnification of about fifty, and a beautiful sight they are. With a higher magnification you may be able to see the dark division in them, but the globe of Saturn is so small that you will probably not see any markings. Binoculars will show its largest moon, Titan, and a small telescope will show several more, but you will need the B.A.A. *Handbook* to identify them.

Uranus and Neptune. You will need the B.A.A. *Handbook* for the charts it gives of the positions of these faint planets. It is very satisfying to find these outer worlds. At the moment, Uranus is in the constellation of Libra (the Scales), and Neptune is in Ophiuchus (the Serpent-bearer), so that they are best seen around May and June, rather low in the southern sky. Uranus can be seen easily with binoculars, but Neptune will probably require a telescope.

Deep-sky objects

With a telescope of sixty to one hundred millimetres in aperture you could spend a happy year of moonless evenings looking at the objects marked in *Norton's Star Atlas*. You will find lists of interesting telescopic objects included with the charts in this book. If you want to look further, get hold of Volume 2 of *Celestial Objects for Common Telescopes*, which is mentioned in Appendix 1. You will find hundreds of double stars, nebulae, clusters and galaxies here, and when you have observed as many as your telescope will reach you will know the sky really well – probably better than most amateur astronomers. You will have left this book far behind, too. The voyage that you are embarking on is about the longest that anyone will ever undertake. Good luck – and good viewing!

Appendix 1
Books and addresses

Every amateur astronomer needs to own a fairly detailed star atlas. The best one to purchase is the *Star Atlas and Reference Handbook* by A. P. Norton (16th edition, 1974), published by Gall & Inglis, Edinburgh. This book shows the position of every naked-eye star in the sky, and also includes lists of interesting objects to observe with small or medium-size telescopes. If you have only a pair of binoculars, my own *Astronomy with Binoculars* (2nd edition, 1976), published by Faber & Faber, contains fairly detailed maps and lists and may be found useful. Volume 2 of *Celestial Objects for Common Telescopes* by T. W. Webb, reprinted by Dover Publications (New York), contains details of many hundreds of objects, and most of them are marked in Norton's *Star Atlas*.

The serious amateur would be hard put to manage without the annual *Handbook* of the British Astronomical Association. This gives details of the movements of the Moon, planets and their satellites, and comets during each year, as well as other information. This can be bought from the Association's headquarters at Burlington House, Piccadilly, London WC1. The national society for young beginners is the Junior Astronomical Society (details from the Secretary, 58 Vaughan Gardens, Ilford, Essex).

However, the best society to join is your local one – if one exists! To find out if there is a society in your area contact the Federation of Astronomical Societies (secretarial address 19 Warren Road, Kirkby-in-Ashfield, Nottingham). Even if there is no astronomical group your local library may know of a scientific society of some sort to put you in contact with a neighbouring amateur astronomer. Most keen amateurs will be only too pleased to offer help and encouragement.

Appendix 2
An astronomical calendar, 1977–1980

As the Earth goes on its yearly course around the Sun, some of the events in the sky can be foretold without any almanac. The Sun is high in the sky in summer, and low in winter. In summer the constellations Lyra, Cygnus and Aquila shine in the night sky; in winter we see Orion, Gemini and their companions. But the movements of the Moon and planets are much more complicated. The bright planets – Venus, Mars, Jupiter and Saturn – are sometimes visible and sometimes not, while Mercury makes only brief appearances. Every now and then the Sun or Moon goes into eclipse. Sometimes a planet passes near a bright star or another planet, making an eye-catching sight. The Moon, too, sometimes passes very near a planet or a star, and may even move in front of it, producing an **occultation**.

It would be impossible to give complete details of everything that will happen in the sky during the next three years or so. The calendar here just mentions some of the most interesting and important events. Approximate times (in GMT) are given as a guide, but more accurate details will be found in the year's B.A.A. *Handbook*, or possibly in a monthly newspaper star column. The maps in these columns usually show the positions of the brighter planets in the sky.

Here is a general outline of the movements of the planets during the period from 1977 to 1980.

Mercury Visible in the *morning* sky in September 1977, August–September 1978, August 1979 and July–August 1980. Visible in the *evening* sky in March 1978, March 1979 and February 1980. At all the elongation times given it will be about 18° away from the Sun, and rising or setting about $1\frac{1}{2}$–2 hours before or after sunrise or sunset. It is worth looking for the planet about a week on either side of elongation times. Elongations when the planet is not well placed are not listed.

Venus Visible in the morning sky at the end of 1977. Passes superior conjunction on 22 January 1978 and moves into the evening sky, reaching greatest elongation on 29 August. It will be low in the sky and rather poorly placed during this time. By 7 November it has moved into inferior conjunction. On 18 January 1979 it will be well placed at morning elongation. After that, it slowly moves back to superior conjunction on 25 August. On 5 April 1980 it will be at evening elongation once more, very well placed for observation. After passing inferior conjunction on 15 June it will be at morning elongation on 24 August, remaining in the morning sky until the end of the year.

Mars Visible in the morning sky until opposition on 22 January 1978. For some months after that it can be followed into the evening sky. Conjunction is due on 20 January 1979, and another opposition occurs on 25 February 1980.

Jupiter Very well placed for several months around opposition time, which will occur on 23 December 1977. The next oppositions are on 24 January 1979 and 24 February 1980.

Saturn Well placed for several months around opposition time, on 16 February 1978, 1 March 1979 and 13 March 1980.

There are also five fairly active meteor showers during the year, and these always happen on the same date from one year to the next. They are included in the calendar, with a note about whether bright moonlight, which interferes with the viewing of most meteors, will interfere. The January Quadrantid meteors fly from a point in Ursa Major (the Great Bear), and can be the most lively shower in the year. They are best seen late in the night, just before dawn.

1977

Sept	5	Mars and Jupiter about $\frac{1}{2}°$ apart
	21	Mercury at morning elongation
	22	Venus and the star Regulus (in Leo) less than $\frac{1}{2}°$ apart
Oct	21	Orionid meteors. Moon low
Nov	3	Saturn and the star Regulus (in Leo) less than 1° apart
Dec	14	Geminid meteors. No Moon
	23	Jupiter at opposition, in Gemini

1978

Jan	3	Quadrantid meteors. Moon rises late
	19	At 7 pm the Moon will be very close to the bright star Aldebaran, in Taurus
	20	Saturn and the star Regulus (in Leo) 1° apart
	22	Mars at opposition, on the border of Gemini and Cancer
Feb	15	The Moon will be approaching the star Aldebaran (in Taurus) in the late evening
	16	Saturn at opposition, in Leo
March	24	Mercury at evening elongation
April	7	Partial eclipse of the Sun at 3 pm
June	4	Mars and Saturn $\frac{1}{10}°$ apart

	12	Mars and the star Regulus (in Leo) less than 1° apart
July	27	Aquarid meteors. Moon rises late
Aug	11–12	Perseid meteors. Moon low
	14	Venus and Mars just over 1° apart
	26	Moon near star Aldebaran (in Taurus) at 3 am
	29	Venus at evening elongation
	31	Venus close to star Spica, in Virgo
Sept	4	Mercury at morning elongation
	16	Total eclipse of the Moon at 7 pm
Oct	3	Venus appears brightest, evening elongation
	19	Moon near star Aldebaran (in Taurus) at 8 pm
	21	Orionid meteors. Moon above horizon
Nov	16	Moon near star Aldebaran (in Taurus) at 5 am
Dec	14	Venus appears brightest, morning elongation
	14	Geminid meteors. Full Moon

1979

Jan	3	Quadrantid meteors. Moon sets early
	9	Moon near star Aldebaran (in Taurus) at 6 pm
	18	Venus at morning elongation
	24	Jupiter at opposition, in Cancer
Feb	5	Moon near star Aldebaran (in Taurus) at 12 pm
	26	Partial eclipse of the Sun, at sunset
March	1	Saturn at opposition, in Leo
	8	Mercury at evening elongation
	13	Partial eclipse of the Moon at 9 pm
July	27	Aquarid meteors. No Moon
Aug	11–12	Perseid meteors. Moon rises late
	16	Moon near star Aldebaran (in Taurus) at 4 am
	19	Mercury at morning elongation
Oct	21	Orionid meteors. No Moon
Nov	6	Moon near star Aldebaran (in Taurus) at 6 am
	13	The Moon and Jupiter less than 1° apart at 7 am
Dec	12	Moon occults Saturn at 5 am
	13	Mars and Jupiter about 2° apart

| | 14 | Geminid meteors. No Moon |
| | 30 | Moon near star Aldebaran (in Taurus) at 12 pm |

1980

Jan	3	Quadrantid meteors. Full Moon
	4	Moon very close to Jupiter at 4 am
Feb	16	Partial eclipse of the Sun at sunrise
	24	Jupiter at opposition, in Leo
	25	Mars at opposition, in Leo
	29	Moon very close to star Regulus (in Leo) at 9 pm
March	2	Moon within $\frac{1}{2}°$ of Saturn at 12 pm
	14	Saturn at opposition, in Leo
	30	Moon within 1° of Saturn at 2 am
April	5	Venus at evening elongation
May	3	Mars and Jupiter about 1° apart
	9	Venus appears brightest, evening elongation
	21	Moon within 1° of Jupiter at 8 pm (daylight)
June	1	Mercury within $\frac{1}{2}°$ of Venus
July	22	Venus appears brightest, morning elongation
	27	Aquarid meteors. Full Moon
Aug	1	Mercury at morning elongation
	11–12	Perseid meteors. No Moon
	24	Venus at morning elongation
Sept	29	Moon near star Aldebaran (in Taurus) at 1 am
Oct	5	Moon near star Regulus (in Leo) at 5 am and Venus at 6 am
Nov	4	The Moon is near Jupiter, Saturn and Venus, all close together in the morning sky
	22	Moon near star Aldebaran (in Taurus) at 10 pm
Dec	14	Geminid meteors. Moon sets early
	26	Moon near star Regulus (in Leo) at 3 am

Much of the information in this appendix was made available
by courtesy of HM Nautical Almanac Office.

Appendix 3 Glossary of astronomical terms

Achromatic lens, used in a refracting telescope, gives a colour-free image. An ordinary, non-achromatic lens will show false colour fringes around the image of a star or planet. An achromatic lens is made by combining two separate lenses.

Altazimuth mounting is the simplest type of stand for an astronomical telescope. One axis lets the telescope move up and down, the other gives a sideways motion.

Altitude is the height of an object above the horizon, measured in degrees.

Aperture is the diameter of the object glass or mirror in a telescope. The larger the aperture, the more light that is collected and the brighter the image.

Aphelion is the point on the orbit of a planet or comet which is furthest from the Sun.

Asteroid is another name for a minor planet.

Astronomical Unit (A.U.) is the name given to the average distance of the Earth from the Sun, 149,600,000 kilometres.

Atoms are arrangements of three basic particles – protons, neutrons and electrons. The elements found in the universe all have different numbers of these particles in their atoms.

Aurora is a glow in the upper atmosphere, usually at a height of between 100 and 1,000 kilometres, caused by particles from the Sun making the thin air luminous.

Binary star consists of two stars revolving around each other.

Celestial sphere is the name given to our view of the night sky as a huge hollow globe, seen from the inside, rotating around the Earth and carrying the Sun, Moon, planets and stars with it.

Centrifugal force tightens the string attached to a whirled stone, or causes the equator of a spinning planet to bulge slightly outwards.

Circumpolar star is one which never sets because it is closer to the Pole Star than the altitude of the Pole Star above the horizon.

Coma is the hazy main body of a comet, surrounding the central nucleus (if any).

Comet is a cloudy body of gas and solid particles orbiting the Sun, usually in a very long and narrow orbit. When close to the Sun it may develop a long tail.

Conjunction occurs when two astronomical bodies (usually two planets) appear close together in the sky. A superior planet, on the far side of the Sun as seen from the Earth, is also said to be in conjunction. (See also inferior and superior conjunction.)

Constellation is a pattern of stars named after a mythical person, animal, or object. The sky is divided into eighty-eight constellations of various sizes and prominence.

Corona is the Sun's atmosphere, extending from its surface for many millions of kilometres.

Cosmos is another word meaning the universe. Cosmogony is the study of how the universe was created, while cosmology is the study of the universe as we see it now.

Declination is used by astronomers to describe the position of an object on the celestial sphere. It is similar to latitude on the Earth's surface.

Dichotomy is the appearance of the Moon, or of the planets Mercury and Venus, when they are at half-phase.

Double star is a pair of stars shining close together in the sky. They may be revolving around each other (binary star), or else be at different distances from the Earth but in almost the same direction (optical double).

Eccentricity is a way of describing the difference between an ellipse and a circle. The more eccentric the ellipse, the more it is flattened into a long, thin loop.

Eclipse happens when the Moon crosses in front of the Sun, cutting off all or part of the Sun's disc (solar eclipse), or when the Moon passes into the shadow of the Sun cast by the Earth (lunar eclipse).

Ecliptic is the path traced out around the celestial sphere by the Sun during the course of the year. This movement of the Sun around the sky is caused by the Earth's movement around its orbit.

Electromagnetic radiation is energy produced by the electrons in an atom vibrating up and down. Radio waves, heat waves, light waves and X-rays are different forms.

Ellipse is the oval form of path in which planets and most comets move. A shape of this sort is said to be elliptical.

Elongation happens when the planet Mercury or Venus is at its greatest distance from the Sun in the sky.

Ephemeris gives the future positions in the sky of a planet, comet or other moving celestial body.

Equatorial mounting, used for astronomical telescopes, has one axis lined up in the same direction as the Earth's axis. Since the Earth spins once a day, turning the telescope around this axis once a day in the opposite direction keeps the telescope pointing at the same direction in space.

Equinox is the moment when spring or autumn begins, usually on 21 March and 23 September (leap years can change the times by a day).

Eyepiece is the small lens or group of lenses to which the eye is placed when looking through a telescope. It magnifies the image formed by the object glass or mirror.

Faculae are very bright clouds of glowing matter in the Sun's atmosphere, usually lasting several days and often seen near sunspots.

Finder is a small aiming telescope fitted to an astronomical telescope.

Fireball is a very bright meteor (brighter than the planet Venus), usually leaving a luminous streak or train that may last for several seconds before fading out.

Flare is an intense outburst of radiation from the Sun's surface. It lasts for only a few minutes, and usually comes from the area of a sunspot.

Flat is the small mirror used in a Newtonian reflecting telescope to reflect the image through a hole in the side of the tube.

Focal length is the distance between a telescope's object glass or mirror and the image it forms of a far-off object, such as the Sun or Moon.

Focal ratio is the number obtained by dividing the focal length of an object glass or mirror by its aperture.

Galaxy is a 'star-city' containing hundreds or thousands of millions of stars.

Globular cluster is a huge swarm of many thousands of stars. About a hundred of these clusters have been found surrounding our Galaxy.

Gravity is a mysterious, universal force which attracts bodies towards each other. The more material there is in a body, the greater its gravitational pull.

Inferior conjunction of Mercury or Venus happens when they pass more or less between the Earth and the Sun. These two worlds are known as inferior planets.

International Astronomical Union (I.A.U.) is an organization of professional astronomers, founded in 1922. It meets in a different country every three years.

Ionosphere is a layer in the Earth's atmosphere between 100 and 500 kilometres high. It reflects radio waves, making long-distance communication possible.

Light-year is the distance travelled by light in one year: 63,240 times the distance of the Earth from the Sun, or 9,460,700,000,000 kilometres.

Limb is the name given to the edge of the Sun, Moon or a planet as it is seen in the sky.

Luminosity is a measure of the amount of light produced by a star. It is usually reckoned in terms of the luminosity of the Sun.

Magnification is the number of times larger an object appears when viewed through a telescope. If it is ten times larger, the magnification is written as 10 × or × 10.

Magnitude is a measure of the brightness of a star or planet.

Main sequence is the family of 'normal' stars to which the Sun and most stars in the Galaxy belong.

Meridian is an imaginary line crossing the sky from the northern to the southern horizon, and passing through the zenith.

Meteor is the streak seen when a tiny interplanetary body about the size of a match-head hurtles through the Earth's atmosphere and burns up.

Meteoroid is the name given to a meteor-producing particle while it is still orbiting the Sun. A meteoroid large enough to land on the Earth's surface is then called a *meteorite*.

Minor planet is one of the group of very small worlds, most of which orbit the Sun between the distances of the planets Mars and Jupiter.

Mirror, with a shallow curved surface, is used in a reflecting telescope to collect the light from the object and form an image.

Moon, see *Satellite*.

Multiple star is a group of three or more stars shining close together in the sky. They may be revolving around each other in space, or else be at very different distances from the Earth but lying in almost the same direction.

Nebula is a cloud of gas or dust inside our galaxy. It may be bright and shining, or be seen as a dark, obscuring patch hiding the stars behind it.

Neutron star is the incredibly dense core which is left after a supernova explosion.

Newtonian telescope forms an image by using two mirrors, one with a concave or hollow face, the other flat. It is the commonest kind of reflecting telescope.

Nova is a star which blasts off its outer layers in a sudden explosion.

Nuclear energy is the energy produced when atoms are broken down and re-formed in a different arrangement.

Object glass is the lens used in a refracting telescope to collect the light from the object and form an image.

Occultation happens when the Moon passes in front of a star or planet. A planet can also occult a star, but this is rare.

Open cluster is a group of a few hundred stars, which split up and become scattered as millions of years pass.

Opera glass is a simple, low-power form of binocular.

Opposition happens when a planet lies opposite to the Sun in the sky.

Orbit is the path followed by one astronomical body revolving around another one.

Ozone is a form of oxygen containing three atoms. A layer of ozone high in our atmosphere cuts out much of the Sun's dangerous high-energy radiation.

Parallax is the shift of a nearby body against a distant background when it is viewed from different positions.

Perihelion is the point on the orbit of a planet or comet which is closest to the Sun.

Penumbra is the outer, lightly shaded region of a sunspot. It is also the hazy edge of a shadow, where the light from the bright object is only partly cut off.

Photosphere is the shining surface of the Sun that we see with the eye.

Planet is a cool, solid body revolving around a star.

Planetarium is an indoor artificial sky, showing the stars and planets projected on the inside of a dome.

Planetary nebula is a round cloud of glowing gas, probably thrown out by a star, which looks like a planet's disc when viewed through a telescope.

Pole Star is the bright star in the constellation of Ursa Minor (the Little Bear) which shines from the direction pointed to by the Earth's north pole.

Pores are dark spots just a few hundred kilometres across on the Sun's surface. They may either die away in a few hours, or develop into a proper sunspot.

Prominence is a huge outburst of glowing material, usually much larger than the Earth, from the surface of the Sun.

Pulsar is the name given to what seems to be a neutron star, usually spinning several times a second and sending out rapid bursts of light and radio waves.

Pupil is the lens opening at the front of the eye. It changes in size according to the brightness of the scene.

Quasar is a mysterious type of object, much brighter than a whole galaxy of stars but apparently much smaller.

Radiant is the point in the sky from which meteors appear to fly during a meteor shower.

Radioactivity is the energy slowly given off when an unstable atom (often uranium) gradually changes into a slightly different form by altering some of its particles.

Red dwarf is a small star, cooler than the Sun and less bright.

Red giant is the swollen, cool star which results when a typical star has turned all its available hydrogen into helium.

Red shift is the way the colour of a shining object (usually a galaxy) becomes redder when it is moving away at a speed of many kilometres a second. An approaching object becomes bluer and shows a *blue shift*.

Reflecting telescope uses a mirror to form its image of the object being viewed.

Refracting telescope uses a lens or object glass to form its image of the object being viewed.

Retina is the sensitive screen at the back of the eye on which the image of the object we are looking at is formed.

Right ascension is used to describe the position of an object on the celestial sphere. It is similar to longitude on the Earth's surface.

Satellite is a small body revolving around a planet. The Earth has one satellite – the Moon – together with a host of man-made ones.

Seeing is a term used by astronomers to describe the state of the Earth's atmosphere, which often makes objects look blurred and trembling when viewed through a telescope.

Shooting star, see *Meteor*.

Sidereal day is the time the Earth takes to rotate once as timed by a star, not by the Sun. It is 23 hours 56 minutes and 4 seconds long.

Sidereal period is the time taken for a planet to revolve around the Sun once, as it would be seen by an observer on the Sun. It is also the time taken for a satellite to revolve once around a planet in relation to the stars.

Sidereal Time (ST) uses a clock regulated to the sidereal day.

Solar day is the time the Earth takes to rotate once as timed by the Sun, not by the stars. This twenty-four hour day is the one used for normal purposes.

Solar System is the family of planets, satellites, meteoroids and comets revolving around the Sun.

Solar wind is the stream of atomic particles poured out by the Sun.

Solstice is the time when the Sun is at its most northerly or southerly point on the celestial sphere. The northerly point (our midsummer day) is reached on 21 June, and the southerly point (midwinter's day) on 21 December.

Spectroscope is an instrument which splits a beam of light into its separate wavelengths or colours. This band is known as a *spectrum*.

Star is a condensed globe of gas shining by its own internal reactions.

Stellar is a way of saying 'to do with the stars' (for instance, stellar astronomy means the study of the stars). Interstellar means between or among the stars (such as interstellar dust clouds).

Sunspot is a patch on the Sun's surface marking the flow of cooler gases, which appear dark because of their lower temperature.

Sunspot cycle is a period of about eleven years during which sunspots are frequent (around 1957 and 1968) and rare (around 1964 and 1976).

Superior conjunction, of Mercury or Venus, happens when the planet is on the far side of the Sun from the Earth.

Superior planet is one with an orbit lying beyond the Earth's (Mars and the outer planets).

Supernova is the destruction of a star in a colossal explosion that seems to leave only the tiny, super-dense core, a neutron star, behind.

Synodic period is the time the Moon or a planet takes to circle the sky once, as seen from the Earth (New Moon to New Moon, for example, and opposition to opposition).

Transit has several meanings, among them the passage of Mercury or Venus across the face of the Sun, or the passage of a satellite, usually of Jupiter or Saturn, in front of the planet. A star, when exactly south, is also said to be in transit.

Twilight is the period between full day, with the Sun above the horizon, and darkness.

Umbra is the cooler and darker central region of a sunspot. It is also the dark centre of a shadow, where all the light from the bright object is cut off.

Universe is the whole system of space, with its countless millions of galaxies, each of which contains thousands of millions of stars.

Volatile substance is a material which easily turns into a gas when heated – such as ice.

Variable star is a star which brightens and fades as seen from the Earth, either because a companion star passes across it or because it really does change in luminosity.

Wavelength is the distance between neighbouring pulses of radiation. In very short-wave radiation (gamma rays) it is less than a millionth of a millimetre, while the wavelength of radio waves can be thousands of metres long.

White dwarf star is believed to be the hot but cooling core of a dying star.

White (or blue) giant is a rare type of star, large and very hot, shining with the strength of thousands of stars like the Sun.

Zenith is the point in the sky directly above the observer.

Zodiac is the region around the sky, about 20° wide, in which the planets are usually to be found.

Zodiacal light is a faint cone of light, caused by sunlight reflected off interplanetary dust, that is sometimes seen extending up from the sunrise or sunset point when the sky is very clear and dark.

Appendix 4 Some new findings

Astromoners have been busy recently. Two *Viking* landers descended on Mars in July and September 1976. On board were instruments to test the soil for living organisms. Nobody was expecting to find anything even as advanced as a plant, because the air is so thin and the temperature so low. Instead, they were looking for microscopic bacteria. Nothing definite was found, but some of the results were unexpected and difficult to explain. No one can yet say definitely that Mars is completely 'dead'; it is *just* possible that simple life-forms of an unknown type exist there.

On 10 March 1977 Saturn ceased to be the only known planet with rings. Uranus, its outer neighbour, passed in front of a star, and astronomers observing this unusual event were amazed to see the star dim and brighten unexpectedly as something invisible – which could only be a faint ring around the planet – passed across it.

Appendix 5 Table of guide stars

The aim of this table is to help you to identify some of the brightest stars in the sky. These 'guide stars' are so important that they have all been given names. In the case of the constellation Orion, however, we simply give the position of his belt – the three stars marking the centre of the constellation. The table gives the name of each star, its constellation, the map or maps on which it is shown highest in the sky, and the details of its passage across the southern direction in the sky.

These times and altitudes are worked out for a place more or less in the middle of the British Isles. However, even if you live in one of the extreme points of the country, these details should be accurate enough to identify the star required because they are all much brighter than any other stars near them.

If you are observing on a different date from those given, remember the 'four minutes earlier each day' rule. For instance, Alpheratz in Andromeda will be due south at 19h GMT (or 7 pm) on the evening of 6 December. If you are observing on 10 December, the star will be due south sixteen minutes (say a quarter of an hour) earlier, or at 6.45 pm. An accuracy of a quarter of an hour or so will be good enough to find these stars.

Star name	Constellation	Map no	Altitude
Alpheratz	Andromeda	6	65°
Mirfak	Perseus	1 and 6	86°
Aldebaran	Taurus (the Bull)	1	52°
Capella	Auriga (the Charioteer)	1	82°
Belt stars	Orion	1	35°
Sirius	Canis Major (the Greater Dog)	1 and 2	19°
Procyon	Canis Minor (the Smaller Dog)	3	41°
Regulus	Leo (the Lion)	2 and 3	48°
Spica	Virgo (the Virgin)	3	25°
Arcturus	Boötes (the Herdsman)	3 and 4	55°
Antares	Scorpius (the Scorpion)	4	10°
Vega	Lyra (the Lyre)	4 and 5	75°
Altair	Aquila (the Eagle)	5	45°
Deneb	Cygnus (the Swan)	5	81°

Day on which the star is south at (GMT)

18h	19h	20h	21h	22h	23h	24h
Dec 22	Dec 6	Nov 22	Nov 6	Oct 22	Oct 7	Sept 22
	Jan 25	Jan 11	Dec 26	Dec 10	Nov 25	Nov 10
	Feb 13	Jan 30	Jan 14	Dec 30	Dec 14	Nov 29
	Feb 22	Feb 8	Jan 24	Jan 9	Dec 24	Dec 8
		Feb 14	Jan 30	Jan 15	Dec 31	Dec 15
		March 2	Feb 16	Feb 1	Jan 17	Jan 1
		March 15	March 1	Feb 15	Jan 31	Jan 15
			April 7	March 23	March 8	Feb 22
				May 18	May 2	April 18
				May 25	May 10	April 25
				June 28	June 13	May 29
			Aug 15	July 31	July 16	July 1
		Sept 17	Sept 1	Aug 18	Aug 3	July 19
	Oct 15	Sept 30	Sept 15	Aug 30	Aug 16	Aug 1

Index

191